Unshakable

Standing Strong When Life Gets Messy

By Monique Lefrancois

Faith Bloom Media

Cover design by Faith Bloom Media
Interior design by Faith Bloom Media

ISBN: 979-8-9945457-0-6
Imprint: Faith Bloom Media

Printed in the United States of America

First Edition

To My Lovely Family—
especially my three amazing girls,
who inspired every word on these pages.

This book was written with you in mind,
and with the hope that you always know
how strong, brave, and unshakable you truly are.

Welcome

Dear Beautiful Girl,

Why This Book, Why Now? Let's be real—life is kind of a lot right now.

Between social media, school pressure, friendships that feel like roller-coasters, and all the noise about who you should be, it's easy to feel like the ground beneath your feet is constantly shifting. You might wonder: *Who am I, really? Does anyone see me? Why does it feel like everyone else has it figured out but me?*

I want you to know something right from the start:
You are not alone. And you were never meant to do this life thing by yourself.

This book is your safe space—a place where we talk about the hard stuff and the holy stuff. We're going to dig into things like anxiety, comparison, friendships, faith, and finding your purpose. But not with fluffy "just have faith" answers. This is the real deal. We'll anchor everything in truth—God's truth—because that's the only thing that can actually hold you steady when the world feels shaky.

You don't have to be perfect. You don't have to have it all together.
You just have to show up—and stay rooted.

Let's get unshakable, together.

With love,

Monique Lefrancois
Monique Lefrancois

JESUS LOVER   AUTHOR   ENTREPRENEUR

Table of Contents

Part 2: Emotions — Finding Peace in the Storm
Managing Feelings Without Letting Them Rule You

Part 4: Living Unshakable
Roadmap Built on Truth, Not Trends

## PART 1

IDENTITY
Who Am I, Really?
Rooting Your Worth in God's Truth

Chapter 1:
The Mirror & the Message

Learning to See Yourself the Way God Does

Let's Be Real...

You know those mornings when you wake up, stumble into the bathroom, and catch a glimpse of yourself in the mirror—and immediately wish you hadn't?

"Wow... I didn't know my hair could defy gravity like that."

Or maybe it's not the messy bun or the toothpaste on your hoodie that gets to you. Maybe it's the way you zero in on your flaws—your skin, your weight, your nose, your height, your everything.

Been there. Way too often.

I remember a time in eighth grade when I begged my mom to let me stay home from school because I had this giant pimple on my forehead. I'm talking Mount Everest status. I was convinced everyone at school would stare at it like it had its own gravitational pull. (Spoiler: they didn't. But I wore a headband that made me look like a backup dancer from a 90s boy band just in case.)

The point is: we're all trying to figure out who we are. And somewhere between selfies, social media scrolls, and society's standards of "beauty," it's easy to feel like we're not enough.

But here's the truth: *You are not what you see in the mirror. You are what God sees in you.*

And His view? Oh girl, it's full of love, purpose, and jaw-dropping worth.

What God Says About You

Let's start with one of the most powerful verses about identity in the entire Bible:

"I praise you because I am fearfully and wonderfully made; your works are wonderful, I know that full well."
—Psalm 139:14 (NIV)

Let's break that down:

"Fearfully and wonderfully made" — That means God made you with intention, awe, and creativity. You're not a mistake, a copy, or a backup version of someone else. You are a custom, handcrafted, one-of-a-kind creation.

"Your works are wonderful" — Yep, that includes you. Not just sunsets, oceans, and baby animals—YOU.

When you stand in front of the mirror, God doesn't see what you critique. He sees His daughter. His masterpiece. His beloved girl with dreams, quirks, talents, and a purpose bigger than you can imagine.

The World vs. The Word

The world says:

"You need flawless skin."

"You have to have the 'right' body type."

"Your worth is based on how many likes you get."

God says:

"You are made in My image." **(Genesis 1:27)**

"You are chosen, holy, and dearly loved." **(Colossians 3:12)**

"You are altogether beautiful, my darling; there is no flaw in you." **(Song of Solomon 4:7)**

So whose voice are you listening to?

The world shouts, but God speaks in a still, steady whisper. It's time to tune into His frequency and let that be the soundtrack to how you see yourself.

A Story You Might Relate To

Meet my friend Jess. She's hilarious, kind, super smart, and loves baking cookies at 2am. But for years, she hated how she looked. She would always crop herself out of pictures, wear baggy clothes to hide her body, and avoid eye contact with mirrors like they were cursed objects.

One day at youth group, the speaker handed everyone a mirror and said, "Look into it. Not to find flaws—but to find your Father's fingerprints." Jess stared at her reflection, tears in her eyes, and whispered, "I am His." That moment didn't magically fix everything, but it was the beginning of healing. She started replacing lies with truth—one verse, one prayer, one brave day at a time.

Now, Jess leads a small group of middle school girls. And you better believe she's the first one cheering them on when they struggle to believe they're enough.

Journal Prompt

Take a few minutes to answer these questions in your journal or notes app:

- o   What do I usually say to myself when I look in the mirror?

- o   Where do those thoughts come from—God or the world?

- o   What would change if I started seeing myself the way God does?

Write out **Psalm 139:14** in your own words—make it personal. Like this:
"God, You made me amazing. Not because I'm perfect, but because You made me on purpose and with love."

This Week's Challenge

For the next 7 days, every time you look in the mirror, say this out loud (or whisper if you're in public and don't want people to think you're talking to your reflection):

"I am fearfully and wonderfully made. I am loved. I am His."

This Week's Challenge: Write it on a sticky note and slap it on your mirror, your laptop, or your water bottle.

Let God's Word be louder than the world's lies.

 Let's Pray

Dear Heavenly Father,

Sometimes it's so hard to see myself the way You see me. I focus on everything I think is wrong, and I forget that I am Your creation—beautiful, chosen, and deeply loved. Help me quiet the lies in my head and replace them with Your truth. Teach me to look in the mirror and see a girl who is fearfully and wonderfully made, just as You say. I want to believe it, live it, and help others see it too. Thank You for making me... me.

In Jesus name,
Amen.

You ready, girl? Let's stop chasing approval and start walking in our God-given identity. Because you were never meant to fit in—you were meant to stand out.

Next stop: we're diving into the world of labels, lies, and those lovely little things called likes. Let's find out what really defines you.

## Chapter 2

Who Do You Think You Are?

Finding Your Real Identity in a World Full of Labels

You know that moment when someone says, "Tell me about yourself," and your brain goes totally blank?

Like… uh, I'm 15, I have a weird obsession with iced coffee, I listen to sad music even when I'm in a good mood, and I'm currently pretending I don't have three homework assignments due tomorrow?

Yeah, identity is tricky.

Because the world throws labels at us like they're on sale at Target. You might hear:

- *You're the smart one.*
- *You're the shy one.*
- *You're the athlete.*
- *You're the pretty one.*
- *You're too much.*
- *You're not enough.*

And sometimes, without realizing it, we start to believe those labels. We wear them like name tags. We let them shape how we see ourselves and how we think God sees us.

But here's the thing: God's definition of you has nothing to do with your social status, your GPA, your looks, or your reputation. He doesn't look at you and see a label—He sees your heart.

The Label Trap

Let me tell you about middle school me (brace yourself). I was the **try-hard**. The straight-A student. The one who volunteered for extra credit even when I didn't need it. And you know what? I let that label define me. If I got a B, I'd spiral. I thought being "the smart one" was the only thing that made me valuable.

One time, I bombed a math test—like, legendary failure. I cried in the bathroom, not because I didn't understand the math (okay, a little because of that), but because I felt like I had failed as a person. That test wasn't just a test—it was proof that I wasn't who I thought I had to be.

That moment taught me something. When our identity is tied to performance, we'll always feel like we're one failure away from not being good enough.

What God Says About You

Let's look at what God says:

"But you are a chosen people, a royal priesthood, a holy nation, God's special possession..."
—1 Peter 2:9a (NIV)

Chosen. Royal. Holy. Special.

These are not temporary titles. They're not things you earn.
They're truths spoken over you by the God who made you.

And there's more:

"See what great love the Father has lavished on us, that we should be called children of God! And that is what we are!"
—1 John 3:1a (NIV)

You are a *child of God*. Not just a face in the crowd. Not just "one of the girls." You are His. Loved on purpose. Chosen on purpose.

Let that sink in. You're not just here to survive high school or make people like you. You were made for something more. For belonging. For purpose. For love that doesn't wear off.

A Story: Lexi's Closet Breakdown

Let me tell you about Lexi. She's the queen of mismatched socks, always
has snacks in her backpack, and never turns in homework on time. One
day, we were getting ready for a youth event, and I walked in on her sitting
in the middle of a mountain of clothes. She looked up at me and said, "I
hate everything in my closet and I hate myself."

Oof.

She wasn't really mad about the clothes. She was tired of trying to be
everyone's version of "cool." She'd changed her style five times in a week,
trying to be sporty, edgy, trendy, you name it. And all it did was make her
feel less like herself.

We sat on that messy floor, and I told her, "You don't have to try so hard
to be what everyone else wants. You get to just be you. And God *likes* that
version."

Lexi wore sweatpants to youth group that night. And she laughed more
than I'd seen in weeks.

Journal Prompt

Take a few minutes and think through these questions. You can write your
answers or just talk to God about them.

- o   What labels have you picked up from other people (good or bad)?

- o   Which labels do you think God would remove if He were sitting
  right next to you?

- o   What would change in your life if you started to see yourself as
  "God's special possession"?

If you want to go deeper, write this out and finish the sentence:

"God, I've believed I'm _____, but You say I am _____."

# This Week's Challenge

Pick one truth God says about you, and speak it over yourself every day. You can choose from the verses above, or find your own. Write it on a sticky note. Put it on your mirror, your phone lock screen, or your notebook.

Say it out loud—yes, OUT LOUD—when you're tempted to label yourself with something less than true.

Need ideas? Try these:

- o "I am God's child."

- o "I am chosen."

- o "I am loved without condition."

- o "I am enough in Christ."

Labels don't define you. Jesus does.

Let's Pray

Dear Heavenly Father,

You know how easy it is for me to believe what the world says about me. Sometimes I feel like I don't measure up, like I'm not who I'm supposed to be. Help me to hear Your voice louder than the labels. Remind me that I'm Yours, that I'm chosen, and that I'm loved beyond measure. Teach me to let go of lies and walk in the truth of who I really am.

In Jesus name,
Amen.

Let's keep this going. You're learning to live unshakable—not because life is easy, but because your foundation is strong. In the next chapter, we're talking about comparison and how to stop letting it steal your joy.

Spoiler alert: You're already enough.

Chapter 3:
Fearfully & Wonderfully Made

Raise your hand if you've ever looked in the mirror and thought:
"Ugh... why am I like this?"

Too loud. Too quiet. Too tall. Too short. Too shy. Too extra.
Not smart enough. Not pretty enough. Not talented enough.

Girl, I see you.
I've been you.
And I want to tell you something that changes *everything*:

"I praise You because I am fearfully and wonderfully made; Your works are wonderful, I know that full well."
— Psalm 139:14

That includes YOU—exactly as you are.

The Battle Against Insecurity

Here's the truth no one talks about: *Almost everyone* feels insecure sometimes. Even the most "put together" girls you see at school or online, have moments where they feel not good enough.

But insecurity is sneaky.
It whispers lies that sound like truth:

- o   "If I looked like her, I'd be happier."

- o   "If I was more outgoing, people would like me."

- o   "If I didn't mess up so much, God could actually use me."

Let's call those lies out right now. Because when you believe you're broken, you forget Who made you. God doesn't mess up. And *He did* not start with you.

You're Not "Too Much" or "Not Enough"

Somewhere along the line, the world started handing out labels like they were party favors:

- o "You're too emotional."

- o "You're not funny enough."

- o "You're too intense."

- o "You're too quiet."

But God says:

"You are My masterpiece." (Ephesians 2:10, paraphrased)

Every personality trait, quirk, and "weird" thing about you?
It's all part of the design.

Your laugh-snort? Designed.
Your love of journaling and deep convos? Crafted on purpose.
Your boldness? Needed.
Your gentleness? Powerful.

You were never meant to be anyone else. You were made to be fully, wonderfully, beautifully you.

Embracing Your God-Given Uniqueness

Let's flip the script. What if instead of wishing you were different, you celebrated who God created you to be?

What if you stopped apologizing for your personality, and started showing up fully and confidently?

What if you believed that the things that make you stand out... are the very things God wants to *shine through*?

Owning your uniqueness isn't prideful—it's powerful.
It's saying, "God, I trust Your design."

Journal Prompt

- o What do I often criticize about myself that God might actually celebrate?

- o Where have I believed I'm "too much" or "not enough"?

- o What are 3 ways God made me unique—and how can I use those gifts for Him?

This Week's Challenge

Write Psalm 139:14 somewhere you'll see it every day—your bathroom mirror, your phone lock screen, or inside your journal.

And next time those "not enough" thoughts try to sneak in? Speak the truth out loud: "I am fearfully and wonderfully made. I'm not a mistake. I'm a masterpiece."

You were fearfully and wonderfully made, not fearfully and almost wonderfully made. God didn't give you the short end of the creativity stick. He handcrafted your heart, your mind, your personality—every bit of you—with love and intention.

So stop comparing.
Stop shrinking.
Start owning your God-given awesomeness.

You're not too much.
You're not too little.
You're just right.

 ## Let's Pray

Dear Heavenly Father,

Help me see myself the way You see me. When I feel insecure, remind me that I was made on purpose and for a purpose. I don't need to change who I am to fit in—I just need to live fully as the girl You created. Help me celebrate the things that make me different, and use them to shine for You.

In Jesus name,
Amen.

## Chapter 4

Body Image & Appearance Obsession

Let's be real—body image is hard. Whether it's your weight, your skin, your hair, your height, or the way your jeans fit—at some point, every girl has looked in the mirror and thought, *"Ugh, why do I look like this?"* It's like the world hands us a measuring tape and dares us to see how we stack up. Beauty becomes a scoreboard, and suddenly, we feel like we're losing.

Everywhere you turn, you're being told your body is your value. From ads to influencers, the message is loud: *"If you looked more like her, you'd be happier. If you were thinner, curvier, taller, prettier—then you'd be worthy."* But chasing that kind of beauty is like chasing the wind. It's exhausting. It's never enough. And it's a lie.

You weren't created to obsess over your appearance. You were created to shine from the inside out.

God's Truth

God sees you differently. He's not scrolling through your selfies judging your angles. He's looking at your heart. While the world's focused on what's visible, God's focused on what's eternal.

1 Samuel 16:7 (NIV) says:
"The Lord does not look at the things people look at. People look at the outward appearance, but the Lord looks at the heart."

That verse flips the script. God isn't impressed by a beauty filter—He's moved by kindness, compassion, honesty, and courage. He sees your worth not because of your waistline, but because you're His.

And even though your appearance doesn't define you, your body does matter—because it's His. According to 1 Corinthians 6:19–20, your body is a temple of the Holy Spirit. That means you're sacred space. You don't have to punish your body to be beautiful—you can honor it because it's a gift from God.

God's version of beauty starts with the soul. It shines through your laughter, your confidence, your love, your faith. That's what makes someone truly radiant—not a flawless face, but a fierce heart that knows who she is in Christ.

 # Key Scriptures

1 Samuel 16:7 (NIV):
"The Lord does not look at the things people look at. People look at the outward appearance, but the Lord looks at the heart."

God's view of beauty is deeper than the mirror. He sees your character. Your motives. Your spirit. And that's what matters most.

1 Corinthians 6:19–20 (NIV):
"Do you not know that your bodies are temples of the Holy Spirit, who is in you, whom you have received from God? You are not your own; you were bought at a price.
Therefore honor God with your bodies."

You were bought with a price. That means you're already valuable—body, mind, and soul. You don't need to change yourself to be loved. You are loved already.

Psalm 139:14 (NIV):
"I praise you because I am fearfully and wonderfully made; your works are wonderful, I know that full well."

You're wonderfully made—not accidentally assembled. Every part of you is intentional. Let that truth drown out the lies.

Living It Out

- o   **Speak kindly to yourself.** No more trash talk when you look in the mirror. Your words matter—especially the ones you say to yourself.

- o   **Don't let the scale, the size tag, or the algorithm decide your worth.** They don't get a say—God already gave you your value.

- o   **Fuel your body with love.** Eat, move, rest, and care for yourself like you actually matter—because you do.

- o   **Look for real beauty in others**—not just in how they look, but in how they love. That's how you train your eyes to see like God.

Journal Prompt

- o   What have I believed about my body that doesn't line up with what God says? Be honest—write down the lies you've picked up from the world, social media, or your own inner critic.

- o   How would my life change if I truly believed I was fearfully and wonderfully made? What would I stop doing? What would I start doing?

- o   What are three things I love about who I am—not what I look like, but who I am inside? Think character, personality, spirit—what makes you shine?

- o   What does it mean to honor God with my body? Describe a few small ways you can start caring for your body out of love, not pressure.

- o   When do I feel most beautiful? Is it when you're laughing with friends?
Worshipping? Helping someone? Pay attention to those moments—God's joy is all over them.

- o   What would I say to a friend who feels the way I do about her body? Now—say those kind words to yourself.

# This Week's Challenge

Stand in front of the mirror this week and speak this truth out loud:
"I am fearfully and wonderfully made. My body is not a problem to fix—it's a temple to care for. I honor God with how I see myself."

Then write down three things you love about who you are—not what you look like, but who you are.

# Let's Pray

Dear Heavenly Father,

I've spent so much time wishing I looked different. I've compared myself, criticized myself, and believed the lie that I'm not enough. But You say I'm fearfully and wonderfully made. Help me see myself through Your eyes—not the world's. Remind me that my beauty isn't based on a number, a filter, or someone else's opinion. It's rooted in You. Teach me to care for my body with grace, not pressure. Let my heart be what shines brightest. And when I'm tempted to believe I'm less than, whisper again that I'm deeply loved.

In Jesus' name,
Amen.

## Chapter 5

Pressure to Be "Too Much" or "Not Enough"

Do you ever feel like you're stuck between two extremes? One moment, culture says, *"Be bold! Be confident! Stand out!"*. The next moment, it whispers, *"Don't be too much. Don't take up too much space. Be quiet. Don't make waves."* It can be confusing trying to figure out where you fit in, especially when everyone seems to have a different opinion on how you should act, speak, or present yourself. One minute you feel like you're too loud, too dramatic, too "extra"... and the next, you're told you're too quiet, too shy, too "invisible."

These conflicting pressures can leave you feeling like you're stuck in an endless balancing act, trying to please everyone and unsure of who you really are. Maybe you've felt like your personality is "too much" for some people to handle, or you've struggled with the feeling that you're not enough of what others expect. You're trying to figure out where you belong, but everything around you keeps sending mixed messages. The truth is, you don't need to conform to someone else's idea of who you should be. God created you exactly as you are, on purpose, with purpose, and your personality isn't something to be fixed or toned down—it's part of His perfect design.

God's Truth

When you try to fit yourself into the world's mold, you'll always feel like you're coming up short—too much or not enough. But God has something better for you: He created you fearfully and wonderfully, and He gave you a personality that's just right for the plans He has for you.

In **Psalm 139:13–16**, David writes about how God made us with intention and purpose: *"For you created my inmost being; you knit me together in my mother's womb. I praise you because I am fearfully and wonderfully made;*

your works are wonderful, I know that full well." God didn't just make you on a whim; He knit you together with a specific plan in mind. Every part of you—your personality, your gifts, your quirks—is part of that plan. The world might say you're too much or not enough, but God says you are exactly as you should be, and that's beautiful.

Jesus Himself didn't fit the mold of what society expected, and He didn't try to please everyone. He was exactly who God called Him to be—bold, loving, confident, and sometimes quiet when He needed to be. In **John 17:4**, Jesus prayed, *"I have brought you glory on earth by finishing the work you gave me to do."* He wasn't focused on being "too much" or "not enough"—He was focused on fulfilling His purpose. And God has a purpose for you too, one that's not about fitting into other people's standards but about living out the unique calling He's placed on your life.

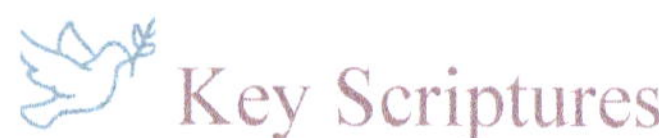 Key Scriptures

Psalm 139:13–16 (NIV):
"For you created my inmost being; you knit me together in my mother's womb. I praise you because I am fearfully and wonderfully made; your works are wonderful, I know that full well."

You are fearfully and wonderfully made. God created every part of you, from your personality to your abilities, for a specific purpose. You don't have to change to fit into a mold; you are already who you were meant to be.

Ephesians 2:10 (NIV):
"For we are God's handiwork, created in Christ Jesus to do good works, which God prepared in advance for us to do."

God has a plan for you—a unique purpose that only you can fulfill. Your personality is part of that plan, and it's meant to shine in the way only you can.

John 17:4 (NIV):
"I have brought you glory on earth by finishing the work you gave me to do."

Like Jesus, your goal isn't to conform to others' expectations—it's to fulfill the work God has for you, and that work is tied to who He created you to be.

 # Living It Out

- o **Embrace who God made you to be:** You don't have to be anyone other than who you are. Embrace the uniqueness of your personality and the gifts God has given you. Don't try to shrink or hide parts of yourself to fit in. You are made in His image, and that's something to be proud of.

- o **Stop comparing yourself to others:** It's easy to look at someone else and think, "I wish I were more like them." But God has given you a distinct role to play in His Kingdom. When you compare yourself to others, you miss out on embracing the specific qualities that make you special.

- o **Focus on God's purpose for your life:** Instead of worrying about how you measure up to others' standards, focus on the work God has prepared for you. Your purpose isn't about being "perfect" in the world's eyes—it's about living in obedience to God's call and fulfilling the unique plans He has for you.

- o **Celebrate your individuality:** Whether you're loud or quiet, bold or reserved, God has a purpose for your personality. Let your authentic self shine, and don't hide or shrink back because of what others may think. God made you exactly how you are for a reason.

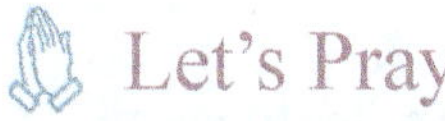 # This Week's Challenge

This week, take time to reflect on how God made you and what unique qualities you bring to the world. Write down three things about your personality or gifts that you used to think were "too much" or "not enough." Now, ask God to show you how those qualities can be used for His purpose.

Let's Pray

Dear Heavenly Father,

Thank You for creating me fearfully and wonderfully. Sometimes, I get caught up in trying to fit into what others expect of me, and I struggle with feeling like I'm either too much or not enough. Help me to embrace who You made me to be and to walk in the confidence that I am Your handiwork. Thank You for the purpose You've placed in my life. Teach me to focus on fulfilling Your plans for me, rather than worrying about what others think. Help me to love and celebrate who I am in You.
In Jesus' name, Amen.

## Chapter 6

Breaking Free from Perfectionism

If there's one thing that might feel like it's been drilled into us by culture, it's the idea that we must be flawless. We see it on social media, in school, in our friend groups, and even from ourselves—this pressure to always be perfect, to never fail, and to constantly perform. The idea that if we make a mistake, we're somehow less than or not good enough. Maybe you stress over every test, every conversation, every post. Maybe you feel like you need to be the best at everything to get attention, validation, or approval.

Here's the problem with perfectionism: it's exhausting. Trying to be flawless all the time leaves you drained and anxious. The truth is, perfection isn't even possible. Everyone has their flaws, their mistakes, and their moments of weakness. But here's the good news—God doesn't call you to be perfect. He calls you to be faithful. And His grace is way bigger than our mistakes.

God's Truth

In **2 Corinthians 12:9**, Paul writes: *"But he said to me, 'My grace is sufficient for you, for my power is made perfect in weakness.' Therefore I will boast all the more gladly of my weaknesses, so that the power of Christ may rest upon me."*

God isn't looking for perfection. He's looking for your heart. His grace is enough to cover our imperfections, and His power is made even stronger in our weaknesses. That's right—God's power shines brightest when we recognize that we can't do it all on our own. You're not meant to be flawless. You're meant to rely on Him, to trust that He is more than enough for every shortcoming you feel.

God calls us to be faithful in what He's given us. Faithfulness means showing up, doing your best, and trusting that He will work through you, even in your mess. Perfectionism is rooted in fear—fear of failing, fear of rejection, fear of not being good enough. But **1 John 4:18** says: *"There is no fear in* *love. But perfect love drives out fear, because fear has to do with punishment. The one who fears is not made perfect in love."* God's love drives out that fear, and He reminds us that we are enough because of Him—not because of how perfectly we perform.

Key Scriptures

2 Corinthians 12:9 (NIV):
"My grace is sufficient for you, for my power is made perfect in weakness"

➡️ This verse is a reminder that God's grace covers our flaws, and His power is made even more evident in our weaknesses. We don't have to be perfect to be used by God—our imperfections make room for His power.

1 John 4:18 (NIV):
"There is no fear in love. But perfect love drives out fear, because fear has to do with punishment. The one who fears is not made perfect in love."

➡️ Perfectionism is rooted in fear—the fear of being rejected, criticized, or not enough. But God's love casts out that fear. When we rest in His love, we don't have to fear failure, because He's already proven His love for us.

Matthew 11:28–30 (NIV):
"Come to me, all you who are weary and burdened, and I will give you rest. Take my yoke upon you and learn from me, for I am gentle and humble in heart, and you will find rest for your souls. For my yoke is easy and my burden is light."

➡️ God doesn't want you to carry the heavy burden of perfectionism. He invites you to come to Him with your weaknesses, your flaws, and your struggles. In Him, you'll find rest, not more pressure.

Living It Out

o **Embrace your humanity:** Remember that mistakes are part of being human. Instead of trying to hide your flaws, acknowledge them and give them to God. Ask Him to use your weaknesses to bring glory to Himself.

- o **Shift your focus:** Instead of striving for perfection, focus on being faithful. Show up with your best effort, but let go of the need for everything to be flawless. Faithfulness is more important than perfection.

- o **Trust in God's grace:** Whenever you start to feel overwhelmed by perfectionist thoughts, remind yourself that God's grace is more than enough. It's not about how perfect you are; it's about how perfect His love is for you.

- o **Practice self-compassion:** Be kind to yourself. Perfectionism often leads to harsh self-criticism. Instead, remind yourself that you are loved by God, flaws and all. You don't have to earn His love through perfection.

This Week's Challenge

This week, every time you feel the urge to be perfect, take a step back and ask yourself: *What is God calling me to right now?* Is it to be flawless, or is it to be faithful? Write down one area of your life where you can let go of perfection and trust in God's grace. Let go of the need to perform and embrace the freedom that comes from being loved as you are.

Let's Pray

Dear Heavenly Father,

Thank You for Your incredible grace. I confess that I often feel the weight of needing to be perfect, and it's exhausting. I try so hard to meet everyone's expectations and to perform flawlessly, but I know that's not what You've called me to. Thank You for reminding me that Your grace is sufficient, and Your power is made perfect in my weaknesses. Help me to let go of the pressure to be perfect and instead to focus on being faithful. Teach me to trust You with my imperfections and to rest in Your love. I am enough because of You, and I choose to believe that.

In Jesus' name, Amen.

## Chapter 7

"Am I Enough?"

Let's be honest—there's a ton of pressure to define yourself by what the world says matters. Whether it's how many followers you have, what clothes you wear, your grades, your body type, or how "put together" your life looks, the world is constantly shouting messages at you like: *"Be prettier." "Be smarter." "Be more popular." "Be perfect."* It's exhausting, right? And the worst part? You can do all those things and still feel like it's not enough. Because the world's definition of worth is always changing—and always demanding more.

But here's the good news: you don't have to play that game. God's definition of you has never changed and never will. You're not defined by your mistakes, your highlight reel, or other people's opinions. You are defined by the One who made you, loves you, and calls you His own.

God's Truth

God doesn't look at what's on the outside—He sees your heart. While the world might measure your worth by appearance, achievements, or popularity, God measures your worth by something unshakable: your identity in Him. He doesn't require perfection; He desires connection. He's not impressed by filters or fame—He's drawn to your faith and your heart.

You don't need to chase after the world's version of success to matter. You already matter. You're already seen. You're already deeply loved. And your life has value—not because of what you do, but because of *whose* you are.

Key Scriptures

Ephesians 2:10 (NIV): *"For we are God's handiwork, created in Christ Jesus to do good works, which God prepared in advance for us to do."*

You're not a random accident. You are God's masterpiece. That means every detail about you—your personality, your laugh, your quirks—was handcrafted with care. And there are good things God's already lined up for you to do. You don't have to chase purpose; you get to walk in it.

1 Peter 2:9 (NIV): *"But you are a chosen people, a royal priesthood, a holy nation, God's special possession, that you may declare the praises of him who called you out of darkness into his wonderful light."*

This verse is a total identity reset. You're chosen. You're royalty. You belong. And your life has a bigger purpose than just getting through the day—you were meant to shine, to speak hope, and to live in the light of God's love.

Romans 8:16–17 (NLT): *"For his Spirit joins with our spirit to affirm that we are God's children. And since we are his children, we are his heirs."*

You're not just in the family—you're an heir. That means you have access to God's promises, His presence, and His power in your life. That's a secure identity no one can take away.

Living It Out

- o **Start speaking truth over yourself.** Write down or say out loud: *"I am loved. I am chosen. I am God's daughter. I have purpose."*

- o **Get to know the One who made you.** Spend time reading His Word (even if it's just a verse a day), and ask Him to show you how He sees you.

- o **Take a break from trying to please everyone.** You weren't made to fit into every mold—just the one God shaped for you.

 This Week's Challenge

This week, every time you catch yourself thinking, *"I'm not good enough"* or *"I don't know who I am,"* pause and ask: What does God say about me? Write that truth somewhere you'll see it every day—your mirror, your phone wallpaper, or your journal.

 Let's Pray

Dear Heavenly Father,

Thank You for creating me with purpose and calling me Yours. Sometimes I feel lost, confused, or like I don't measure up. But I choose to believe what You say about me over what the world says. Help me to see myself the way You do—loved, chosen, and enough because of You. Teach me to walk confidently in my identity as Your daughter and to let go of the pressure to be someone I'm not. I want to know You more, trust You deeper, and live like I truly belong to You.

In Jesus name,
Amen.

## Chapter 8

Success & Future Pressure

Have you ever felt the weight of the world on your shoulders, like you need to have it all figured out right now? It's like everyone around you has a plan, and they're moving forward with confidence while you're just trying to figure out what comes next. Whether it's about choosing a career, picking a college, deciding who to hang out with, or figuring out where your life is headed, the pressure to succeed can feel overwhelming.

Culture constantly bombards you with messages that tell you to hustle, to be the best, to achieve more, and to have everything planned out perfectly. "Your future depends on what you do right now," the world says. It feels like if you don't have all the answers and the perfect plan for your life, you're falling behind. There's so much pressure to get it right, to have your future mapped out and your success guaranteed.

But here's the truth: You don't have to have it all figured out. It's okay not to know exactly what's coming next. In fact, trying to control your future and feeling like you need to figure it out all on your own can be exhausting. The good news? You don't have to carry that burden. God's got it. And He's more than capable of leading you through the unknowns of life.

God's Truth

In **Proverbs 3:5–6**, we are reminded, *"Trust in the Lord with all your heart and lean not on your own understanding; in all your ways submit to him, and he will make your paths straight."* Notice that it doesn't say, "Figure everything out yourself," or "You need to have a perfect plan." It says **trust in the Lord** and submit to His guidance, and He will make your paths straight.

God knows your future better than you do. He has a plan for your life, and it's far better than any plan you could create on your own. It's not about figuring everything out right now; it's about trusting that God is with you every step of the way and that He is directing your steps, even when you can't see the whole picture.

Sometimes, the pressure to succeed can make you feel like you have to know exactly where you're going. But God doesn't ask you to have all the answers. He asks you to trust Him, to walk in faith, and to rely on His guidance as you move forward. **Success isn't about having it all figured out; it's about trusting the One who does.**

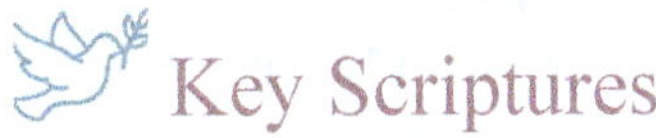 Key Scriptures

Proverbs 3:5–6 (NIV):
"Trust in the Lord with all your heart and lean not on your own understanding; in all your ways submit to him, and he will make your paths straight."

Your job isn't to have it all figured out. Your job is to trust God and let Him lead you.

Jeremiah 29:11 (NIV):
"For I know the plans I have for you," declares the Lord, "plans to prosper you and not to harm you, plans to give you a hope and a future."

God has good plans for you, even when the future seems uncertain. His plans are full of hope and promise.

Psalm 37:23–24 (NIV):
"The Lord makes firm the steps of the one who delights in him; though he may stumble, he will not fall, for the Lord upholds him with his hand."

Even if you stumble along the way, God will uphold you and guide you through. Trust Him with every step.

Living It Out

- o **Trust God with your future:** It's easy to feel like you have to have a clear vision of your future, but trusting God means letting go of the need to control everything. When you surrender your dreams, fears, and uncertainties to God, He promises to direct your steps. Instead of stressing about what you don't know, choose to focus on what you do know: God is good, He loves you, and He will lead you exactly where you need to go.

- o **Take one step at a time:** The future may feel overwhelming, but you don't have to have it all mapped out. Break it down into smaller steps. Focus on the next decision or action you need to take. God promises that He will make your path straight. You don't need to see the whole staircase; just trust Him for the next step.

- o **Embrace the unknown:** Sometimes the fear of not knowing what's next can paralyze us. But the unknown is not something to fear; it's an opportunity to see God work in ways we couldn't have planned. Embrace the adventure of walking by faith and not by sight.

- o **Remember, success is trusting God, not achieving perfection:** The world will tell you that success is about perfect grades, perfect looks, and perfect accomplishments. But God defines success differently. It's not about being perfect—it's about being faithful. It's about trusting Him with your future, even when you don't have all the answers.

This Week's Challenge

Take some time to reflect on the future pressure you feel. What areas of your life are causing you the most stress or uncertainty? Write down any fears or doubts you have about your future, then surrender them to God. Ask Him to help you trust Him more fully and to guide you in the decisions you need to make. Take a step today to walk by faith, not by sight.

 Let's Pray

Dear Heavenly Father,

Thank You for the promise that You are with me every step of the way. I confess that sometimes I feel overwhelmed by the pressure to figure everything out. It's hard to trust the future when it feels so uncertain. But today, I choose to surrender my worries and my plans to You. I trust that You have a good and hopeful plan for my life, and I want to walk in Your will, not my own. Help me to take one step at a time and to trust You with my future. I know that You will make my path straight, and I trust that You will lead me to the places You have prepared for me. Thank You for Your peace and guidance.

In Jesus' name,
Amen.

## Chapter 9

Identity Confusion (Who Am I?)

It's one of the most common questions we ask ourselves as teens: *"Who am I, really?"* It seems like everyone has an answer except for us. You might look around and see people constantly reinventing themselves to match the trends—changing their hair, their style, their opinions, their personalities. Everyone seems to have a different version of who they are, and you might feel like you're caught up in trying to figure it all out. One minute, you feel confident and sure of yourself, and the next, you question everything. Maybe you're trying to fit in with your friends, or you're tempted to change things about yourself to meet society's standards.

But here's the thing: Your true identity isn't something you have to create or change based on what's popular or who you're with. It's not about chasing after a version of yourself that's constantly changing. Your identity is a gift. It's not something you have to earn or invent—it's something you get to receive from the One who created you.

God's Truth

When it comes to defining who we are, we don't have to look to the trends or the opinions of others. We can look to God. He is the one who created us, and He's the one who defines us. The world says, *"Define yourself however you want."* But God says, *"I've already defined you."*

In **1 Peter 2:9,** the Bible tells us: *"But you are a chosen people, a royal priesthood, a holy nation, God's special possession, that you may declare the praises of him who called you out of darkness into his wonderful light."*

God's truth is powerful and liberating: You are chosen. You are loved. You are called. You are set apart. You are not a random collection of traits or a result of your circumstances. You are deeply and intentionally made by a Creator who knows you inside and out.

God calls you *His*—not because of your performance or your ability to fit into the world's standards, but because He created you and declared you valuable. In **Ephesians 2:10**, it says: *"For we are God's handiwork, created in Christ Jesus to do good works, which God prepared in advance for us to do."*

You are His masterpiece, created with purpose and intention. Your identity is a gift that God has already given you—it's not something you have to search for or manufacture. It's not about being "whatever you want to be." It's about receiving the identity He's already given you and walking in it.

Key Scriptures

1 Peter 2:9 (NIV):
"But you are a chosen people, a royal priesthood, a holy nation, God's special possession, that you may declare the praises of him who called you out of darkness into his wonderful light."

This verse affirms who you truly are in God's eyes. You are chosen, set apart, and called to declare His praises. You are not defined by the trends, but by your Creator.

Ephesians 2:10 (NIV):
"For we are God's handiwork, created in Christ Jesus to do good works, which God prepared in advance for us to do."

You are God's masterpiece, created with purpose. Your identity is already designed by Him, and He has a plan for your life. You don't have to chase an identity—God has already made you who you're meant to be.

Jeremiah 29:11 (NIV):
"For I know the plans I have for you," declares the Lord, "plans to prosper you and not to harm you, plans to give you a hope and a future."

This verse shows that God has a plan for your life. He knew you before you were even born, and He has designed a purpose for you that's beyond anything the world can offer. Your identity is secured in His plan.

Living It Out

- o **Remember who you are:** Every time you're faced with a choice about your identity—whether it's something you post on social media, the way you dress, or how you act—ask yourself, "Is this reflecting who God says I am?" You are chosen, loved, and set apart, so live like it.

- o **Stop chasing trends:** The world constantly tells you to change who you are to fit in. But the truth is, trends will come and go, and you'll be left wondering who you really are. Instead of chasing after the next big thing, root yourself in the truth of who God says you are.

- o **Embrace your uniqueness:** You don't have to be like everyone else. God made you with a unique purpose, and you're not supposed to fit into someone else's mold. Embrace the gifts, talents, and personality He has given you.

- o **Spend time with God:** The more you know Him, the more you understand your true identity. Take time every day to pray, read His Word, and ask Him to show you who you are in Him.

This Week's Challenge

This week, every time you feel unsure about who you are, pause and remind yourself of these truths from God's Word: *You are chosen. You are loved. You are His masterpiece.* Write down three things that make you unique and give thanks to God for making you exactly the way you are. Whenever you feel the pressure to fit into someone else's mold, ask yourself, What does God say about me?

Let's Pray

Dear God,

Thank You for creating me on purpose and with purpose. The world around me constantly tells me to change, to fit in, and to be someone I'm not. But I know that You have already defined me. I am chosen. I am loved. I am Your masterpiece. Teach me to embrace who You've made me to be and to walk confidently in my identity as Your daughter. Thank You for loving me just as I am.

In Jesus' name, Amen.

## Chapter 10

Sexual Identity, Purity & God's Design

Have you ever felt like the world is telling you that your sexual identity is something to explore, experiment with, and define however you want? Culture bombards you with messages about love, sex, and relationships that often feel confusing or overwhelming. It seems like everyone is telling you to explore your desires, to push boundaries, and to define love and intimacy on your own terms. There's this pressure to figure it out for yourself, but sometimes it feels like everyone else is doing it with such confidence, while you're left wondering what's actually healthy, true, and lasting.

The world says, *"Sex is just a way to have fun. Explore it freely. Don't let anyone tell you what's right or wrong. Love is love, and it's whatever you decide it is."* It's easy to get caught up in this mindset, but deep down, you might feel like something's missing—like there's more to love and intimacy than what culture is offering. Maybe you've even been hurt or confused by relationships in the past, and now you're unsure of what purity really means or how to honor your body and your heart in the way God intended.

The truth is, God has something far better for you. He created love and sex as beautiful, sacred gifts, meant to be enjoyed in the context of marriage. And if you've made mistakes or struggled with past choices, there's good news: God offers forgiveness and a fresh start through Christ. Your worth isn't tied to your past; it's rooted in who you are in Him.

God's Truth:

God designed sex to be a gift for marriage, a beautiful expression of love that reflects His covenant with His people. In **1 Thessalonians 4:3–5**, Paul writes: *"It is God's will that you should be sanctified: that you should avoid sexual immorality; that each of you should learn to control your own body* *in a way that is holy and honorable, not in passionate lust like the heathen, who do not know God."* Sexual purity is not about denying a good gift; it's about honoring God's design for it. In His plan, sex is not just physical—it's deeply emotional and spiritual, meant to bond a husband and wife in a covenant that mirrors Christ's relationship with the Church.

When we follow God's plan, we protect ourselves from the emotional and spiritual wounds that often accompany premature or unhealthy relationships. And here's the thing: *Your worth is not defined by your past mistakes.* If you've made choices that have hurt you or others, you don't have to carry that shame forever. In 2 Corinthians 5:17, we're reminded, *"Therefore, if anyone is in Christ, the new creation has come: The old has gone, the new is here!"* You are made new in Christ. No matter what your past looks like, God offers forgiveness, healing, and a fresh start. His love is not based on what you've done but on who He is and what He has done for you.

Sexual purity is not about perfection—it's about walking in alignment with God's purpose for your life. It's about honoring your body, respecting your heart, and seeking God's best for your relationships. *Purity is not a punishment; it's a path to freedom and blessing.*

 # Key Scriptures

1 Thessalonians 4:3–5 (NIV):
"It is God's will that you should be sanctified: that you should avoid sexual immorality; that each of you should learn to control your own body in a way that is holy and honorable, not in passionate lust like the heathen, who do not know God."

Sexual purity is God's will for your life. It's not about restriction, but about aligning yourself with His design for healthy, holy relationships.

2 Corinthians 5:17 (NIV):
"Therefore, if anyone is in Christ, the new creation has come: The old has gone, the new is here!"

No matter what your past looks like, you can experience a fresh start in Christ. You are a new creation, free from guilt and shame.

Hebrews 13:4 (NIV):
"Marriage should be honored by all, and the marriage bed kept pure, for God will judge the adulterer and all the sexually immoral."

God honors marriage, and sexual purity is part of that honor. Sex is meant to be celebrated in the context of a committed, loving marriage.

Living It Out

o **Embrace God's design for love and intimacy:** The world might say that love is about following your feelings and exploring different relationships. But God's design for love and sex is a beautiful reflection of His covenant with us. When we live according to His plan, we protect our hearts and honor His gift of intimacy. Remember that purity is not about restriction, but about freedom—freedom to experience the deepest and most fulfilling relationships in God's timing.

o **Know your worth:** Your worth is not based on your past mistakes, nor is it determined by how many relationships you've had or how many people have affirmed you. You are loved and accepted by God, just as you are. No matter where you've been, God offers a fresh start and the chance to walk in His grace.

o **Set boundaries that honor God:** Setting boundaries in relationships isn't about controlling others; it's about honoring yourself and your relationship with God. If you are dating or thinking about dating, ask yourself how you can honor God with your body, your heart, and your emotions. Surround yourself with people who support your decision to live according to God's plan.

o **Focus on healing and growth:** If you've struggled with purity in the past or feel weighed down by guilt, know that God offers complete forgiveness. Take time to heal, seek counsel if needed, and allow God to restore your heart. Remember, His grace is greater than any past mistakes.

 # This Week's Challenge

Think about the relationships and choices you've made in the past. Are there areas where you need healing or forgiveness? Take a moment to surrender those areas to God and ask for His grace to help you move forward in purity. Consider setting specific boundaries in your current or future relationships that honor God and reflect His love. Take time to pray, asking God to help you walk in the freedom He offers through sexual purity.

Let's Pray

Dear Heavenly Father,

Thank You for creating me with purpose and for designing love and intimacy in a way that reflects Your beauty and holiness. I confess that at times, I've allowed the world's definition of love and sex to shape my choices. But today, I choose to surrender my past and my future to You. I ask for Your for-giveness for any mistakes I've made, and I receive the fresh start You offer through Christ. Help me to honor You with my body and my relationships. Give me the strength and wisdom to set boundaries that protect my heart and reflect Your holiness. Thank You for the gift of purity and for the freedom that comes with following Your plan.

In Jesus' name,
Amen.

## PART 2

EMOTIONS
Finding Peace in the Storm

Managing Feelings Without
Letting Them
Rule You

Chapter 11:

Anxiety & Overthinking

Finding Peace When Your Thoughts Are Loud

Have you ever had a moment where your mind just won't shut off?

Like, you're lying in bed at 11:47 p.m. and your brain is like, "Hey, let's replay that awkward thing you said at lunch... from 4 years ago." And suddenly, you're spiraling. Overthinking. Imagining 147 ways something could go wrong.

Yup. Been there. Too many times.

Anxiety is one of those things that doesn't always look like hyperventilating into a paper bag (though sometimes, it feels close). Sometimes it looks like overthinking every text message. Or feeling nervous for no reason. Or trying to plan everything so nothing goes wrong. It's exhausting.

Story Time: The Backpack Breakdown

Let me take you back to 10th grade. I was juggling too many things—school, youth group, volleyball practice, trying to keep up a social life (which basically meant replying to memes in group chats), and pretending I had it all together.

One day, my backpack strap broke in the middle of the school hallway. It should've been a "laugh it off" moment... but I lost it. Like, crying-in-the-bathroom-stall lost it.

The truth is, it wasn't about the backpack. It was the final crack in a dam that had been ready to burst. I had been carrying way too much—not just books, but pressure, expectations, fears, what-ifs, and self-doubt. My anxiety had been building, quietly, until it screamed for attention.

Here's what God says to that anxious, overwhelmed, can't-stop-worrying heart:

"Do not be anxious about anything, but in every situation, by prayer and petition, with thanksgiving, present your requests to God."
—Philippians 4:6 (NIV)

 God's not saying, "Just stop being anxious, already!" He's saying, *Bring it to Me.* Every situation. Every stress. Every late-night panic spiral. He wants it.

And then this:

"And the peace of God, which transcends all understanding, will guard your hearts and your minds in Christ Jesus."
—Philippians 4:7 (NIV)

Peace that doesn't even make sense? Yes, please.

God's peace isn't just a calm feeling. It's a guard. Like a bodyguard for your heart and mind. It shows up when your world doesn't make sense. When you *should* be panicking, but instead you're standing steady because God's holding you close.

What Helps When You're Anxious

Let's get practical for a sec. Here are a few things that actually helped me when anxiety felt like it was winning:

- o **Breathe on purpose.** (Yeah, I know—you already breathe. But try slowing down. Inhale peace. Exhale stress. It's weirdly powerful.)

- o **Write it out.** Anxiety is messy in your head but makes more sense on paper. I'd scribble my worries in a notebook and hand them to God, one by one.

- o **Speak truth out loud.** Verses. Prayers. Gratitude. Even if your voice shakes. Sometimes your heart needs to hear what your head already knows.

- o **Tell someone.** A trusted friend, leader, or parent. You don't have to carry it alone. Seriously, you're not a bother. You're human.

 Journal Prompt

Grab your journal or open your notes app and be real with God:

- o   What's been making you anxious lately?

- o   When does anxiety show up the most for you?

- o   What would it look like to give those fears to God—really give them?

Now finish this sentence in your own words:

"God, I'm afraid of _____, but I choose to trust You with it because You are _____."

 This Week's Challenge

This week, create a "Peace Plan." Pick one thing you'll do when you start to feel anxious. It could be:

- o   Praying out loud, even if it's just "God, help me."

- o   Quoting a verse like Philippians 4:6-7.

- o   Taking five deep breaths and thanking God for five things.

- o   Going for a quick walk and playing worship music.

Anxiety doesn't vanish overnight—but every time you turn to God instead of spiraling, you're building peace muscle. And that's a pretty amazing strength.

Let's Pray

Dear Heavenly Father,

You know every thought before I even think it. And still, You never back away. You draw near. I'm tired of pretending I have it all together. I need Your peace—the kind that guards my heart and mind when nothing else makes sense. Help me trust You with every fear, every unknown, and every what-if. Remind me that I'm not alone, even when I feel overwhelmed. You are with me, and You are for me.

In Jesus' name, Amen.

## Chapter 12

Depression, Sadness & When Life Feels Heavy

Let's talk about something real—something heavy. Depression. Maybe you don't call it that. Maybe you say you're just tired all the time, or that you feel numb, or like there's a dark cloud hanging over you that you just can't shake. Maybe you cry and don't know why... or maybe you can't cry at all, and you wonder if that means something's wrong with you.

Sometimes depression feels like you're underwater, struggling to breathe while everyone else around you is splashing and smiling in the sunshine. You try to come up for air, but the weight pulling you down feels too strong. You might wonder: *Where is God in this? Why do I feel this way? Is something wrong with my faith because I feel so low?*

If that's where you are right now, take a deep breath. First, you're not alone. Second, you're not broken. And third, depression doesn't make you less loved by God. In fact, He sees you in the struggle and wants to walk with you through it—not around it.

Yes, even in the darkest, loneliest places, God is there. Psalm 34:18 tells us, *"The Lord is close to the brokenhearted and saves those who are crushed in spirit."* God doesn't shame you for your pain. He sits with you in it. He doesn't rush you to "get over it"—He walks with you step by step toward healing and hope.

God's Truth

Depression is not a sign of weak faith. It's a sign that you're human. Even strong, faith-filled people in the Bible experienced deep sorrow and overwhelming sadness.

David, the man after God's own heart, cried out in **Psalm 42:11**, *"Why, my soul, are you downcast? Why so disturbed within me?"* Elijah, one of the most powerful prophets, begged God to take his life because he was so overwhelmed **(1 Kings 19)**. And Jesus—yes, Jesus—wept and felt deep anguish **(Luke 22:44)**.

God doesn't dismiss your pain—He enters into it with you. And here's the beautiful truth: depression doesn't get the final word over your life. God does. And He says that you are His, that you are loved, and that you are never alone. He invites you to bring your whole heart—hurts and all—into His presence.

Healing may not always come in an instant. Sometimes it's a journey, with prayer, support, counseling, and small steps forward. And that's okay. Depression doesn't define you. God does—and He calls you chosen, cherished, and whole in Him.

 Key Scriptures

Psalm 34:18 (NIV)

"The Lord is close to the brokenhearted and saves those who are crushed in spirit."
God isn't distant when you're hurting—He's closer than ever. He draws near, not away, in your lowest moments.

Psalm 42:11 (NIV)

"Why, my soul, are you downcast? Why so disturbed within me? Put your hope in God, for I will yet praise him, my Savior and my God."
Even when your soul feels heavy, you can speak truth over your feelings—hope in God is still real, even when it feels far away.

Isaiah 41:10 (NIV)

"So do not fear, for I am with you; do not be dismayed, for I am your God. I will strengthen you and help you; I will uphold you with my righteous right hand."
God promises strength when you feel weak. You don't have to carry the weight alone—He's holding you up.

1 Kings 19:4–8 (NIV)

Elijah asked that he might die… but God gave him rest, food, and encouragement.
Sometimes what we need most isn't a quick fix—it's rest, nourishment, and reassurance that we're not alone.

Living It Out

Here are some gentle, practical ways to take care of yourself when you feel like you're drowning:

o   **Talk to God honestly.**
    You don't need to clean up your feelings to talk to God. Pour it all out—your sadness, your confusion, even your anger. He can handle it. In fact, He welcomes it.

o   **Ask for help.**
    You weren't meant to walk through this alone. Talk to a trusted adult, a counselor, a mentor, or a doctor. Needing help isn't weakness—it's wisdom and courage.

o   **Take care of your body.**
    Small steps matter. Try to sleep, eat nourishing food, take a short walk, or sit in the sunshine. These things don't "fix" depression, but they can help gently support your healing.

o   **Surround yourself with truth.**
    Write down encouraging scriptures. Listen to worship music. Journal your prayers. When your mind is clouded, the truth of God's Word can be an anchor.

o   **Be kind to yourself.**
    Healing takes time. You don't have to rush it. You're allowed to have bad days. God isn't in a hurry, and He's not disappointed in you. He's walking with you, patiently and lovingly.

Journal Prompt

o   What does depression feel like for you? Try putting your emotions into words, even if they don't come out perfectly.

o   Have you ever felt like God was far away during a tough time? What do you want to say to Him right now?

o   What are three things that bring you comfort or peace, even on the hard days? How might those be small ways God is caring for you?

# This Week's Challenge

This week, choose one small step to care for yourself—whether that's reaching out for help, reading a Psalm each day, taking a walk, or simply getting some rest. Remind yourself that healing isn't about "fixing" yourself—it's about letting God hold you while you heal.

You are not drowning alone. The One who walks on water is with you in the storm.

# Let's Pray

Dear Jesus,

Sometimes the weight I'm carrying feels too heavy. I try to smile, but inside I feel like I'm barely holding it together. I don't always understand why I feel this way, but I know You see me—even in the dark.

Thank You for never leaving me, even when I feel lost, numb, or overwhelmed. Thank You for being close when my heart is broken. I don't have all the answers, but I'm choosing to believe that You are with me, and that You care about every part of my story—including this part.

Help me take the next step, even if it's small. Give me strength when I feel weak. Bring people into my life who will walk with me and remind me of Your love when I forget. Help me be kind to myself while I heal, and help me rest in the truth that I'm never alone.

You are my anchor when the waves feel too strong. Hold me close, God. I need You.

In Jesus' name,
Amen.

## Chapter 13

Stressed Out & Spiraling

Ever feel like your brain has 347 tabs open and you forgot which one was playing the music? Yeah, welcome to the club.

Stress. It creeps up when your to-do list is five miles long, your phone won't stop buzzing, and you've got finals, practice, youth group, chores, and a group text that needs a response now. Oh—and let's not forget the pressure to look put together while pretending none of this is bothering you. (Spoiler: it is.)

Let me tell you about the time i almost cried over a sock.

Okay, so one night, after a long day of school, studying, and trying to be everything for everyone, I got home and couldn't find the other sock to my favorite pair. Just one lonely sock. And I lost it. I sat on the floor of my closet crying like my whole life had fallen apart. But it wasn't about the sock. It was about the pressure building up all week. That sock was just the final straw.

Stress does that. It piles up silently—until even the tiniest thing sends us into a tailspin. But god never asked you to carry it all.

Here's what God says about that:

"Come to me, all who are weary and burdened, and I will give you rest."
—Matthew 11:28 (NIV)

Take a second and really let that soak in. God isn't standing there with a clipboard of expectations. He's offering you rest. A safe place to breathe. An open invitation to hand Him your stress, your panic, your everything.

Jesus doesn't ask us to fake being okay. He just asks us to come to Him as we are—mess, stress, mismatched socks and all.

What Stress Says vs. What God Says

<u>What Stress Says</u>	<u>What God Says</u>
"You'll never get it all done."	*"My grace is sufficient for you."* **(2 Corinthians 12:9)**
'You have to be perfect."	*"You are fearfully and wonderfully made."* **(Psalm 139:14)**
"Everyone else has it together."	*"Come to Me and I'll give you peace."* **(John 14:27)**

So What Do You Do With the Stress?

Here's what helps me (when I remember to slow down and do it):

o   **Pause.** Literally stop what you're doing. Close your eyes. Breathe in. Breathe out. Again.

o   **Pray.** Don't worry about sounding "holy." Just talk to God. Tell Him what's freaking you out.

o   **Prioritize.** Not everything needs to be done today. Ask: "What's actually urgent?"

o   **Power Off.** Social media break? Yes please. That app can wait. Your peace matters more.

o   **People.** Call a trusted friend, leader, or parent. You're not meant to carry it alone.

Journal Prompt

Take out your journal or notebook and reflect on this:

o   What are 3 things causing you stress right now?

o   Which one do you need to give to God today?

o   How does knowing He offers you rest change how you feel about it?

Write them down. Then, draw a little box around the one you're handing over to Him. (You can even write "God's to-do list" at the top if you're a visual girl like me!)

 This Week's Challenge

Try taking 15 minutes each day this week to rest intentionally. That might mean reading your Bible, taking a walk, journaling, listening to worship music, or just being quiet. No screens. No noise. Just you and Jesus.

Keep a sticky note somewhere that says: "I don't have to do it all—Jesus is with me."

Let's Pray

Dear God,

I'm tired. I feel stretched and overwhelmed by so much, and sometimes I don't even know where to start. I need Your peace to calm my racing thoughts and Your strength to carry what I can't. Help me let go of what's not mine to carry. Thank You for offering rest when I feel like I'm drowning. Teach me how to pause, breathe, and trust that You're in control. I give You my stress, and I take Your peace instead.

In Jesus' Name,
Amen.

You're doing better than you think, girl. Stress doesn't have to run your life. God's got you—even when everything feels like too much. Especially then.

You don't have to hustle for peace. It's already yours in Him.

## Chapter 14

Burnout & Trying to Do It All

Have you ever felt like you're just... stuck?

Like you're in a room full of people, but somehow, you're completely alone? Like the world's moving at its usual pace, and you're the only one standing still?

Yeah, me too. It's like your emotions are stuck on pause, and no one around you understands why things just feel heavy.

The Mask We Wear

A few years ago, I was in that exact place. On the outside, everything looked normal. I laughed at jokes, posted pictures on social media, and went through the motions like any other teen. But inside? It felt like I was walking through thick mud, with this weight on my chest that wouldn't go away. No one knew. No one understood.

I didn't want to admit that I was struggling because—honestly—what did I have to be sad about? I had friends, I had a family, I wasn't failing school. But despite all that, I felt completely empty. You know what? It's okay to feel like that. It's okay to not have all the answers. And it's definitely okay to ask for help when it feels like everything's too much.

When You Feel Like You're Not Enough

Sometimes depression makes us feel like we're not good enough, or like we're invisible. I remember looking at my social media feeds and seeing all these perfect lives—friends at cool parties, influencers with their flawless

selfies, people laughing. It made me feel even more like I didn't belong.
But here's the truth that I've had to learn: *You are enough*. Not because
of anything you've done, not because you've got everything together, but
because God says you are.

"You are precious in my sight, and honored, and I love you."
—Isaiah 43:4

God sees you. And He doesn't see the mess or the heaviness you're carrying—
He sees your heart, your worth, and your beauty, even when you don't feel
it yourself.

What to Do When Everything Feels Heavy

When depression hits, it's easy to feel like it's never going to get better. The
days drag on, and the feelings of sadness or emptiness seem endless. But
remember, you don't have to stay stuck.

Here's how I've learned to take baby steps toward healing:

- o **Acknowledge Your Feelings:**
  You don't need to bottle everything up. It's okay to admit when
  you're feeling off, and it's okay to not have all the answers right
  away. Giving yourself permission to feel what you feel is powerful.

- o **Reach Out:**
  When I was going through my own struggle, I learned the hard
  way that talking about it helps. Whether it's a close friend, a
  parent, or a counselor, don't keep it inside. It can feel scary, but
  once you speak the words, you'll realize you›re not alone.

- o **Lean Into Prayer:**
  When everything feels heavy, talking to God has been a
  game-changer. You don't have to have a fancy prayer—just talk to
  Him like you would to a friend. He's already there, ready to listen.

- o **Take Care of Your Body:**
  Depression often shows up in our physical bodies—tiredness,
  headaches, tension. Try to get enough sleep, eat foods that make
  you feel good, and move your body. It doesn't have to be a full
  workout—just going for a walk can do wonders.

o   **Find Something That Brings You Joy:**
    Even on the tough days, try to find something, anything, that
    gives you a little spark of joy. It could be watching your favorite
    show, reading a book, journaling, or even drawing. Just some-
    thing that's for you.

You Are Not Alone

Girl, you are never alone in this. Yes, you may feel lonely at times or like no
one really understands. But remember this: God sees you, loves you, and is
with you every step of the way. You don't have to stay stuck in the darkness,
and you don't have to pretend you're okay when you're not.

You are precious to God. He cares about every part of you—even the
messy parts. Keep taking those small steps toward healing. God's with you
in every single one.

You are enough. You are loved. You are not alone.

Journal Prompt

Grab your journal and reflect on this:

o   What's one thing that's been weighing on you lately?

o   What would it look like to give that thing to God today?

o   Write down three things you're thankful for, even if they seem
    small.

Sometimes, just reminding yourself of what you have—even in the hard
times—can shift your perspective.

# This Week's Challenge

This week, commit to reaching out to someone you trust (whether it's a friend, a family member, or a mentor) and let them know you're struggling. It's not about fixing everything right away—it's about being real and asking for support. You're not meant to carry this alone.

# Let's Pray

Dear God,

I come to You with a heart that feels heavy and a mind that's spinning. Sometimes it's hard to see past the sadness, but I know You're always there, ready to listen. Help me to remember that I don't have to pretend everything's fine. I don't have to carry this on my own. Thank You for loving me even when I don't feel like I deserve it. Please heal my heart and fill me with Your peace. Help me to feel Your presence and to remember that I am enough, just as I am.

In Jesus' Name,
Amen.

## Chapter 15

Battles of the Mind

The War We Don't Always See

You're scrolling through your feed. That girl has the perfect hair. Another's on a dream vacation. Someone else just made the varsity team... and there it is—that sinking feeling. It starts small. A whisper: *"You're not enough."* Then more: *"She's prettier than you. Smarter. More liked."* Before you know it, you're tangled in a thought spiral of comparison, jealousy, overthinking, and straight-up self-criticism.

We've all been there. These battles may be quiet, but they are fierce. And guess what? You are not weak for having these thoughts. But you are powerful when you learn to fight back—with God's truth.

"We take captive every thought to make it obedient to Christ."
— 2 Corinthians 10:5b (NIV)

Let's break that down together.

This verse is like a spiritual game plan for your thought life. Paul—the writer this letter—wasn't just talking to adults with deep theology degrees. He was writing to everyday people who were wrestling with what they believed and how to live it out. Sound familiar?

"Take captive" literally means to *seize, arrest, or take control of something.* Imagine you're a thought detective. When a lie pops into your mind— like *"I'm not good enough"*—you don't just let it hang around. You **grab it**, question it, and put it on trial.

If it doesn't line up with what Jesus says about you?

It. Has. To. Go.

"Make it obedient to Christ" **means** *aligning your thoughts* **with what Jesus says in His Word. It's like asking,** *"Is this thought something Jesus would want me to believe?"*

If not, then it's not your truth—it's just background noise trying to mess with your peace.

This verse reminds you that your mind isn't a free-for-all. With God's help, *you're in charge of what gets to stay and what gets shown the door.*

"Finally, brothers and sisters, whatever is true, whatever is noble, whatever is right, whatever is pure, whatever is lovely, whatever is admirable—if anything is excellent or praiseworthy—think about such things."
— Philippians 4:8 (NIV)

Have you ever noticed how quickly your mind can spiral? One insecure thought turns into a flood of comparison. One embarrassing moment replays like a highlight reel on repeat. One comment from a friend becomes a full-blown story in your head about how you're "too much" or "not enough."

This verse? It's God's mental reset button.

Let's break it down piece by piece, because each word is an intentional checkpoint from God to protect your peace:

"Whatever is true"
Ask yourself: *Is this thought based on truth—or just fear or assumption?*

That "I'm not good enough" feeling? Not true. God says you're chosen, loved, and made on purpose **(1 Peter 2:9, Ephesians 2:10)**.

Truth matters. If it's not real, don't let it rule.

"Whatever is noble"
Noble means honorable, worthy of respect.

Think about things that elevate you instead of things that drag you down. Gossip? Not noble. Obsessing over what someone else thinks of you? Not noble. Let your thoughts reflect your royalty as a daughter of the King.

"Whatever is right"

This is about *righteousness*—thinking in line with what God says is right and good.

If the thought is mean-spirited (even if it's about yourself), it's not "right." Reroute your mind toward kindness, forgiveness, and hope.

"Whatever is pure"

Purity isn't just about outward actions—it starts in the mind. Pure thoughts build up your heart, your confidence, and your spirit.

It's about choosing to dwell on things that aren't corrupted by jealousy, bitterness, or shame.

"Whatever is lovely"

Lovely thoughts bring peace, not chaos. Think of what inspires joy, gratitude, and beauty.

When you catch your brain spiraling into worst-case scenarios, pause and choose to refocus on what is *lovely*—like a moment you felt loved, a blessing in your day, or the beauty of God's creation.

"Whatever is admirable"

Is this something worth looking up to? Would you want someone else to know what you're thinking?

Let your thoughts be filled with the kind of stuff that builds courage, compassion, and grace.

"If anything is excellent or praiseworthy"

This is like the cherry on top—if it's excellent or gives God praise, let your heart marinate in it.

There's so much negativity in the world. This is a call to intentionally fix your mind on the good. Not to ignore pain—but to stay anchored in hope.

Here's the truth: You won't always catch a negative thought before it shows up. But you can choose what you let stay.

It's like standing at the door of your mind and saying, "Only life-giving thoughts get in." When something negative sneaks through, ask yourself:

- o   Is this true?

- o   Is this helpful?

- o   Is this what God says about me?

If the answer is no—then it's time to hit delete and replace it with truth.

Truth Talk: Thoughts Can Lie

Let's be honest—our minds can sometimes be mean girls.
They tell us we're behind, not enough, too much, or too broken.

But God? He calls us chosen, beloved, equipped, forgiven, and deeply loved. When we start to compare ourselves or beat ourselves up, here's what we can do:

- o   Catch the thought (Is this something God would say about me?)

- o   This Week's Challenge the lie (Where's the proof? Where's the grace?)

- o   Change the narrative (Speak truth—His truth—over it)

Truth to Replace the Lies:

Toxic Thought	Truth from God
I'll never be as good as her	*"I praise You because I am fearfully and wonderfully made."* **(Psalm 139:14)**
I always mess everything up	*"His mercies are new every morning."* **(Lamentations 3:23)**
I'm too broken	*"He makes all things new."* **(Revelation 21:5)**
No one really sees me	*"You are the God who sees me."* **(Genesis 16:13)**

 # Journal Prompt

- o   Write down three negative thoughts you've had recently.

- o   Now, next to each one, write a truth from God's Word that replaces that thought.

Bonus: Put one of those truths on a sticky note where you'll see it every morning—like your mirror or locker.

 # This Week's Challenge

Pick one "toxic thought" you struggle with the most. Every time it pops up this week, say out loud:

"Nope. I take this thought captive. I replace it with truth."

Then speak a truth verse right after it.

You'll be amazed how your mindset starts to shift.

Let's Pray

Dear Heavenly Father,

You know every thought that runs through my mind—even the ones I'm too ashamed to admit. Thank You for loving me through them. Help me recognize lies quickly and replace them with truth from Your Word. Give me strength to take every thought captive, and peace to believe I am who You say I am.

In Jesus' Name,
Amen.

## Chapter 16

Wrestling with Doubts

"Faith isn't the absence of doubt—it's choosing to trust even when the questions are loud."

The Roller Coaster of Faith

Let's be honest: sometimes faith feels like a mountaintop—everything makes sense, prayers are answered, and your heart feels full of Jesus.

And then there are the valleys.

The days when your prayers feel like they're bouncing off the ceiling. When you look around and wonder why God is silent. When your Bible collects dust because it just doesn't feel relevant anymore. Or when something hard happens, and suddenly your heart whispers: "If God is good... then why?"

If that's where you are right now, I need you to know something right off the bat:

You're not broken. You're not a bad Christian. And God isn't mad at you for asking questions.

Faith was never about having it all figured out—it's about learning to trust in the middle of the mystery.

Faith + Doubt = Growth?

You might think that doubt is the opposite of faith—but it's not.

The opposite of faith is fear that refuses to hope.

Doubt, on the other hand, is more like a doorway. You can choose to walk through it and discover a deeper, more authentic faith on the other side—

or you can sit in it and let it fester into disbelief.

Even the strongest believers wrestled with doubt. Think of:

o   Thomas, who literally said, *"I won't believe until I see the scars for myself"* **(John 20:25)**.

o   David, who cried out, *"Why, Lord, do you stand far off?"* **(Psalm 10:1)**.

o   Job, who lost everything and questioned why God would allow such pain.

And yet—they weren't rejected. They were invited closer.

Ask the Hard Questions

Here's the truth: God is not intimidated by your questions.

He *welcomes* them. He is not fragile. He's not waiting to strike you down for saying, *"God, I don't get it."* He's the kind of Father who leans in and says, "I see your questions. I hear your heart. Let's walk through this together."

So go ahead—ask:

o   Why do bad things happen?

o   Why didn't God answer my prayer the way I hoped?

o   Is He really listening?

o   How do I know the Bible is true?

You don't need to hide your doubts in the dark. Bring them into the light— and let God meet you there.

Key Verse: **Jude 1:22**

"Be merciful to those who doubt."

Whoa. Did you catch that? Doubt isn't something to shame. It's something to respond to with mercy. If God calls us to be merciful to those who doubt, don't you think He treats you the same way? You're not falling apart. You're growing roots.

Strength in the Struggle

Think of your faith like a muscle. Doubt is like the weight that. The resistance you feel? It's actually helping you build strength. Here's what happens when you wrestle through doubt:

o   You get to know who God really is, not just who others say He is.

o   You start to ask deeper questions, and your understanding grows.

o   You learn to walk by faith, not just by feelings.

And girl—feelings will come and go. But truth? That's unshakable.

 Key Scriptures

2 Corinthians 12:9 (NIV)

"My grace is sufficient for you, for my power is made perfect in weakness."
    When you feel weak in your faith, that's when God shows up strongest. His grace doesn't depend on your performance. It just is.

Isaiah 55:8–9 (NIV)

"For my thoughts are not your thoughts, neither are your ways my ways," declares the Lord. "As the heavens are higher than the earth, so are my ways higher than your ways and my thoughts than your thoughts."
    When life doesn't make sense, remember: God sees the whole story. He's still writing yours.

Proverbs 3:5–6 (NIV)

"Trust in the Lord with all your heart and lean not on your own understanding; in all your ways submit to him, and he will make your paths straight."
    You don't have to *understand* everything to trust God. You just have to lean on Him.

Okay, first—this verse is one of those classic "fridge magnet" scriptures. You've probably seen it on Pinterest boards, journals, and cute coffee mugs. But let's take a moment to really dig into it. Because this isn't just a pretty verse—it's a lifeline.

"Trust in the Lord with all your heart..."

This is asking you to *let go* of control. Not a half-hearted, "I trust you, God… kind of…" but a full-on surrender.

All your heart means trusting God not just when things are easy, but when they're confusing, scary, or painful.

It's trusting Him when:

You didn't get the part you prayed for in the school play.

Your friendships are rocky and you feel left out.

You're anxious about your future and nothing feels certain.

This kind of trust is not about feeling good all the time. It's about believing God is still good—even when life isn't.

"...and lean not on your own understanding..."

Our understanding? It's limited. We see only a tiny piece of the puzzle. We're down on the ground trying to figure things out while God's up above—seeing the full picture from beginning to end.

Leaning on your own understanding is like trying to put IKEA furniture together without the instructions. It might looklike you're making progress, but eventually, you're going to hit a moment where nothing fits, and frustration hits hard.

This verse says, "Hey—you don't have to figure everything out on your own. Lean on Me instead."

"...in all your ways submit to Him..."

That word *submit* can feel kind of intense, right? But it's not about losing your voice or blindly following. It's about inviting God into every part of your life—not just Sunday mornings or late-night prayers when you're overwhelmed.

"In all your ways" means:

- o   In your relationships

- o   In your schoolwork

- o   In your social media

- o   In your decisions about your future

- o   In your insecurities and doubts

It's saying, *"God, I want You to lead. Even when I don't get it. Even when it's hard."*

"...and He will make your paths straight."

Now, this doesn't mean life will be easy. This verse isn't promising smooth roads with zero bumps or detours.

But it is promising direction. Clarity. Peace. Purpose.

When you let God lead, He takes the winding, confusing path and makes it *clearer.* Maybe not all at once. Maybe not with flashing neon signs. But step by step, He shows you where to go—and more importantly, *who you're becoming along the way.*

Real Talk

God isn't asking you to ignore your questions or pretend life is easy. He's asking you to trust Him more than your fears. More than your doubts. More than your feelings on the hard days.

This verse is your anchor. Your compass. Your reminder that even when life feels crooked and confusing—He knows where you're going. And He's not leaving your side.

 ## Journal Prompt

Write down three honest questions you have for God right now. Don't filter them. Be real. Then, write a prayer asking Him to meet you in those doubts and give you understanding—even if the answers take time.

 ## This Week's Challenge

This week, choose *one moment of doubt* and talk to God about it. Not a polished prayer. Just you, being real. Something like:

"God, I don't get this. It's hard to trust right now. But I'm still here. Help me believe again."

Then look for ways He shows up—through Scripture, a song, a conversation, or even just a quiet sense of peace.

Let's Pray

Dear Heavenly Father,

I don't always understand what You're doing. Sometimes it's hard to trust when everything feels uncertain. But I don't want to run from You—I want to run toward You. Help me be honest with my doubts, and meet me right in the middle of them. Give me wisdom, peace, and a deeper faith, even when things don't make sense. Thank You that I don't have to have perfect faith to be perfectly loved.

In Jesus' name,
Amen.

Chapter 17:
Facing Fear with Faith

Ever had one of those moments when your heart races
and you feel like your mind is about to explode from worry?

Maybe it's an upcoming test, a presentation in front of your class, or maybe it's just the fear of not measuring up to everyone else. You can feel it in your chest—this tight, uncomfortable feeling, like something is about to go horribly wrong. And suddenly, all your thoughts are consumed by what could happen... but most of it is *totally made up in your head.*

Fear is real. It feels like a weight you can't shake off, and sometimes, it makes you question everything. Why am I afraid? What if things go wrong? What if I fail?

I've been there. Fear used to rule my life. I'd get nervous before big events, and even the smallest things would send me spiraling into worry. I r emember the first time I had to speak in front of a group of people—I was so afraid I would say something dumb, or worse, forget everything I had prepared. I could feel the fear building up in my chest, like my body was betraying me. It wasn't just nerves—it was full-on terror.

But here's the thing about fear: it's often louder than the truth. It makes you believe lies about yourself and your abilities. And when we let it take over, it can steal our peace and leave us doubting who we are. But there's a way out, and it's not about pretending the fear isn't there—it's about learning to face it with faith.

The Power of God's Peace

The Bible talks a lot about fear. Over and over, God tells us not to be afraid. It's almost like He knew that fear would be one of our biggest battles, especially for us as teenagers. Whether it's fear of failure, fear of what people think, or fear of the unknown, God wants to help us overcome it. In Isaiah 41:10, He promises:

"So do not fear, for I am with you; do not be dismayed, for I am your God. I will strengthen you and help you; I will uphold you with my righteous right hand."
—Isaiah 41:10

When I read this verse, I'm reminded that fear is *not* something we have to carry alone. God is with us in every moment, and He will strengthen us through it. We don't have to face our fears with our own strength—His strength is enough.

What Fear Really Is

Let's talk about fear for a second. Fear doesn't just exist in the form of big, obvious things like speaking in public or riding a roller coaster. Sometimes, it's subtle—it's the fear of not being good enough or the fear of disappointing the people around you. It's the worry that something bad is going to happen, even when there's no real reason for it. Fear tries to make us believe that we're not strong enough, capable enough, or worthy enough. But here's the truth:

You are enough. You have what it takes.
God has equipped you with everything you need to handle whatever comes your way. Fear can't steal your potential, no matter how loud it gets.

How to Overcome Fear

The first step to overcoming fear is recognizing it for what it is: a liar. It tries to tell you that you're powerless, that you can't do it. But God's Word says something completely different. Let's break down a few steps to help you face your fears head-on:

- o **Acknowledge the Fear:**
  Ignoring fear won't make it go away. When you feel fear, acknowledge it. Say to yourself, *Okay, I'm afraid right now. But I know I don't have to let it control me.*

o **Remember Who You Are in Christ:**
    Fear thrives when we forget who we are. You are a daughter of
    the King, fearfully and wonderfully made. God has called you to
    live a life of courage and boldness. You don't have to shrink back
    because of fear.

o **Speak Truth Over Fear:**
    Fear loves to spread lies. So, combat those lies with the truth
    of God's Word. When fear says, *You're not good enough, God
    says, You are fearfully and wonderfully made (Psalm 139:14).
    When fear says, You can't do it, God says, You can do all things
    through Christ who strengthens you* **(Philippians 4:13)**.

o **Pray and Trust God:**
    The best weapon against fear is prayer. When you feel scared, talk
    to God. Tell Him what you're afraid of and trust that He is in control.
    And remember, He's with you every step of the way, guiding you
    with His peace.

o **You Are Not Defined by Your Fears**

o Fear may show up, but it doesn't get to define you. You are more
    than the things you're afraid of. You are brave, strong, and capable
    of doing all that God has called you to do. So, when fear comes
    knocking, stand tall and say, *Not today. I've got God on my side.*

o **You are not alone in this.** God has already given you the strength
    to face whatever comes your way—fear doesn't stand a chance
    when you stand in His love.

You Are Not Defined by Your Fears

Fear may show up, but it doesn't get to define you. *You are more than the
things you're afraid of.* You are brave, strong, and capable of doing all that
God has called you to do. So, when fear comes knocking, stand tall
and say, *Not today. I've got God on my side.*

You are not alone in this. God has already given you the strength to face
whatever comes your way—fear doesn't stand a chance when you stand in
His love.

# Journal Prompt

Let's take a moment to journal about your fears and how you can face them with God's strength:

- o What is something that you're afraid of right now?

- o How does that fear make you feel?

- o What Bible verse can you stand on to fight this fear?

- o Write a prayer asking God to help you trust Him more and face your fears with faith.

# This Week's Challenge

This week, identify one fear you want to face and take a step toward it. It might be as small as speaking up in class or trying something new. But take that step in faith, knowing that God is with you. The goal isn't to do it perfectly—it's to trust God in the process and let Him help you.

Let's Pray

Dear God,

I know that fear can be so overwhelming at times, and sometimes I feel so small in the face of it. But I also know that You are bigger than any fear I face. Help me to trust You when fear tries to take over. Remind me that You are with me, that I am not alone, and that You've given me everything I need to be brave. Thank You for Your peace that calms my heart and for Your strength that carries me through.

In Jesus' Name,
Amen.

## Chapter 18

Trusting God in the Unknown

Has anyone else ever felt like the future is a huge question mark?

Like, you're standing on the edge of a cliff, looking out over this giant, blank space, and you have no idea what's coming next? Whether it's figuring out what you want to do after high school, making big decisions about friendships, or even just the uncertainty of how your day will go—life can sometimes feel like one big unknown.

I remember when I was in your shoes, about to start high school. I had zero idea what to expect. I was terrified about meeting new people, making new friends, and figuring out how to survive those *awkward first weeks*. It was all so overwhelming, and the fear of the unknown made my mind go into overdrive. *What if I don't fit in? What if I fail? What if I don't live up to everyone's expectations?* **Sound familiar?**

But here's something I've learned through those years of uncertainty: *You don't have to have it all figured out right now.*

Trusting God in the unknown isn't about knowing every single detail or having a perfect plan. It's about believing that He does have a plan—even when we can't see it yet—and that He's got us. He is faithful to guide us through every step, no matter how unclear or uncertain things may seem.

The Fear of the Unknown

One of the hardest parts about trusting God is when you can't see where you're going. The unknown is scary, right? You can feel like you're wandering in a fog, with no clear direction. I totally get it.

I remember when I had to decide what to do after high school. Everyone around me seemed so sure of their paths. *Some were going to college, others* *to work, some even taking a gap year to trave*l. Meanwhile, I was over here, like, *Am I the only one who has absolutely no idea what I'm doing?*

And that's when I realized: *God isn't asking me to have all the answers.* He's asking me to trust Him—step by step. Not knowing exactly what the future holds is tough, but God doesn't expect us to walk alone.

In Proverbs 3:5-6, God gives us a really solid reminder:

"Trust in the Lord with all your heart and lean not on your own understanding; in all your ways submit to Him, and He will make your paths straight."
—Proverbs 3:5-6

This verse is a game-changer. It doesn't say, *Trust in the Lord with your half-hearted effort or trust only when you can see where you're going.* No, it says all your heart. And then it goes on to promise that when you trust Him with everything, He'll make your path straight.

It's like when you're driving in the dark—just because you can't see the end of the road doesn't mean you stop driving. You trust that the road will take you where you need to go, even if you can't see the destination yet.

The unknown feels like an empty canvas, and it's so tempting to try to fill it in with our own plans, right? But God doesn't just leave us in the dark. He's the light, and He'll lead us if we let Him.

Isaiah 55:8-9 gives us some clarity about God's plans for us:

"For my thoughts are not your thoughts, neither are your ways my ways," declares the Lord. "As the heavens are higher than the earth, so are my ways higher than your ways and my thoughts than your thoughts."
—Isaiah 55:8-9

This verse reminds us that God's plan for us is so much bigger and better than anything we could come up with on our own. We might not understand why things happen the way they do, or why we have to wait for certain things, but God's perspective is far beyond ours.

I know it's not always easy to trust God when the future feels so uncertain. It can be hard when everyone around you seems to have everything figured out, and you're still trying to figure out what your next step is. But trust me, *God isn't just concerned with the destination; He's shaping you through the journey.*

How to Trust God When the Future Is Uncertain

1. **Let Go of the Need to Control Everything:**
    This one is hard, but it's true. When we try to control everything, we miss out on letting God lead. It's like trying to steer a car while someone else is driving. Let go and let God take the wheel.

2. **Focus on Today:**
    Stop stressing about next year, next month, or even next week. God gives us what we need for today. Matthew 6:34 says:

    "Therefore do not worry about tomorrow, for tomorrow will worry about itself. Each day has enough trouble of its own."
    —Matthew 6:34

    Just take it one step at a time. You don't have to have the whole year planned out right now. You just need to focus on what God's calling you to do today.

3. **Pray for Peace and Trust:**
    Trusting God in the unknown requires a peace that only comes from Him. Philippians 4:6-7 is such a beautiful reminder of this:

    "Do not be anxious about anything, but in every situation, by prayer and petition, with thanksgiving, present your requests to God. And the peace of God, which transcends all understanding, will guard your hearts and your minds in Christ Jesus."
    —Philippians 4:6-7

    When you feel overwhelmed with the unknown, pray and give it to God. Trust that He will give you the peace you need to move forward.

Journal Prompt

Take a moment to reflect on the areas of your life where you feel uncertain about the future. Write out your feelings and thoughts.

- o   What are the things you're afraid of when you think about the future?

o   How can you trust God more in these areas?

o   Write a prayer asking God to guide you and give you peace in the unknown.

This Week's Challenge

This week, whenever you feel anxious or uncertain about the future, stop and pray. Ask God for the strength to trust Him with each step. And remind yourself that He has a plan for you—one that is better than anything you could ever imagine.

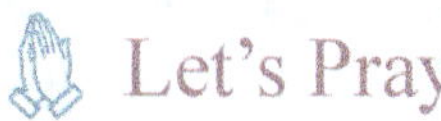

Let's Pray

Dear God,

It's so hard not knowing what the future holds. Sometimes I feel overwhelmed by all the unknowns, and I'm afraid of what might happen. But I know that You are in control, and You have a plan for me. Please help me trust You more and take one step at a time. When I get anxious, remind me of Your promises, and give me Your peace. Thank you for always being there, even when I don't know what's coming next.

In Jesus' Name,
Amen.

Trusting God is a Journey

Remember, you don't have to have the entire picture figured out today. Trusting God in the unknown is a journey, and you're never walking it alone. He's right beside you, guiding you step by step. Keep walking in faith, and you'll see how His plan unfolds in ways you could never imagine.

## Chapter 19

Overcoming Insecurity

Hey girl, I get it. Insecurity can feel like a heavy weight, something that creeps up on you in the most unexpected ways. Maybe it's the way you look in the mirror and wish you could change a few things. Or maybe it's the feeling that you're not good enough compared to those around you. Either way, insecurity can be a tough thing to handle, but you don't have to carry it alone.

I remember a time when I felt really insecure. It was freshman year of high school, and I remember comparing myself to the girls around me who seemed to have everything together. Their hair was always perfect, their outfits were on point, and they seemed to have all the friends. Meanwhile, I was still figuring out how to use a straightener without burning myself (spoiler: I still don't totally get it). I felt like everyone around me had this secret that I wasn't privy to. And honestly? It was hard not to let that make me feel less than.

But here's the thing: You were created on purpose, by a God who loves you exactly as you are. When we compare ourselves to others, we forget that our value doesn't come from how we look or how many friends we have or even what we do on social media. It's about who God says we are. And He's always been the One with the best view of us — the one who sees everything and still calls us "good." Isn't that amazing?

Let's start by taking a look at some Bible truths to remind us of who we are in God's eyes.

Key Scriptures

1. **Psalm 139:14 (NIV):** *"I praise you because I am fearfully and wonderfully made; your works are wonderful, I know that full well."*

    This verse is a game-changer. God didn't make any mistakes when He created you. He carefully designed you to be exactly who you are. So, that quirky laugh you have, or the way your hair always seems to defy gravity? It's all part of His master-piece. When you feel insecure, remember that God doesn't make mistakes — He makes you. And you are fearfully and wonderfully made.

2. **Ephesians 2:10 (NIV):** *"For we are God's handiwork, created in Christ Jesus to do good works, which God prepared in advance for us to do."*

    This verse reminds us that we are God's handiwork — not just a random collection of traits, but a unique design with a purpose. Your value doesn't come from your achievements or how you measure up to others; it comes from the fact that God created you with a purpose only you can fulfill. You don't have to be anyone else because you're exactly who He needs to do the work He's called you to.

3. **2 Corinthians 12:9 (NIV):** *"But he said to me, 'My grace is sufficient for you, for my power is made perfect in weakness.' Therefore I will boast all the more gladly of my weaknesses, so that the power of Christ may rest upon me."*

    In moments when you feel weak or insecure, God's power is most evident. It's easy to want to hide our flaws and insecurities, but when we embrace them, we open the door for God's strength to shine through. It's not about being perfect — it's about embracing His grace in our imperfection. And that's where true strength lies.

Journal Prompt

Now, take a moment and grab a journal. Let's reflect on the times you've felt insecure and how you can start to reframe those thoughts.

o   Write down one thing about yourself that you're insecure about (maybe it's your appearance, your social status, or even your talents).

o   Now, write down a truth from the Bible (or any positive affirmation) that counters that insecurity. For example, if you feel like you're not enough, remind yourself that God says you are fearfully and wonderfully made **(Psalm 139:14)**.

o   Finally, write down one thing you can do today to remind yourself that you are beautifully created, loved by God, and capable of great things. Maybe it's a small act of kindness toward yourself or celebrating one of your unique traits.

This Week's Challenge

This week, I want you to do something that might feel a little uncomfortable but will help break the cycle of insecurity: *Start affirming yourself daily*. This could be as simple as saying out loud, "I am fearfully and wonderfully made," or "I am loved by God just as I am." You might feel silly at first, but don't let that stop you. In fact, the more you say it, the more you'll start to believe it. Words are powerful, and reminding yourself of the truth every day will help shift your mindset over time.

Also, pay attention to how you talk to others. Are you quick to compliment and build others up? In doing that, you'll find that it's easier to embrace your own worth, too.

Let's Pray

Dear God,

Thank You for creating me with purpose and love. Thank You for seeing me as I am — not through the lens of my insecurities, but through the eyes of grace. I pray that You help me to embrace who I am, imperfections and all. Remind me of my worth in You, and help me to see myself the way You see me. When I feel insecure, I pray that I turn to You for strength and truth. Help me to love and appreciate myself more each day. Thank You for making me exactly who I need to be for Your purposes.

In Jesus' name, Amen.

<h1>Chapter 20:
When You Feel Invisible</h1>

Feeling left out, overlooked, or lonely
You're never alone—how God sees and knows you

Have you ever walked into a room and felt like no one even noticed? You're there, but it's like you're not. Maybe your texts go unanswered. Your friends make plans—but forget to include you. Or maybe you're in a crowded place but still feel completely alone.

Feeling invisible hurts. It leaves you wondering, Does anyone see me? Do I even matter? Maybe you've poured yourself into friendships, only to be left behind when something "better" came along. Or you've tried to speak up, only to be talked over or brushed aside.

Loneliness doesn't always mean being physically alone—it's that ache in your heart when you feel unseen, unnoticed, and forgotten. And when that feeling lingers, it can start to chip away at your sense of worth.

But here's something that's 100% true—even if you feel invisible to the world, you are never invisible to God.

God's Truth

God doesn't miss a single detail about you. He doesn't overlook your pain, your tears, or the quiet battles you're fighting inside. He sees you in the moments when no one else does. You are fully known, deeply loved, and never, ever forgotten.

In Genesis 16, there's a powerful story about a woman named Hagar. She was mistreated and cast aside, so she ran into the wilderness—alone, broken, and feeling completely invisible. But God found her. He called her by name.

He saw her. And in that moment, she gave God a new name: *El Roi*, which means "the God who sees me."

You are seen by the same God. El Roi sees your heart. He sees when you're left out. He hears every unspoken hurt and catches every single tear.

Psalm 139:1–3 says,

"You have searched me, Lord, and you know me. You know when I sit and when I rise; you perceive my thoughts from afar. You discern my going out and my lying down; you are familiar with all my ways."

You are never hidden from God's sight. Even when the world scrolls past, God leans in. He knows your heart. He delights in who you are. And when you feel like no one sees you, He does—and He cares more deeply than anyone ever could.

 # Key Scriptures

Genesis 16:13 (NIV)

"She gave this name to the Lord who spoke to her: 'You are the God who sees me,' for she said, 'I have now seen the One who sees me.'"

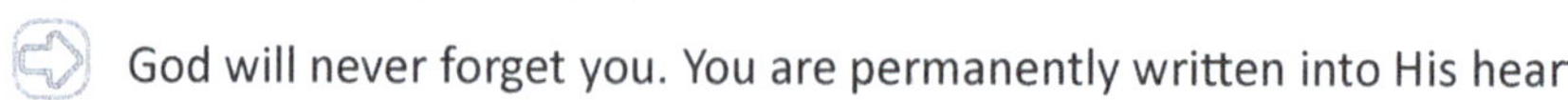 God saw Hagar in her pain, and He sees you too. You are never out of His sight.

Psalm 139:1–3 (NIV)

"You have searched me, Lord, and you know me. You know when I sit and when I rise; you perceive my thoughts from afar."

God knows you intimately—your routines, your thoughts, your feelings. You are not alone.

Isaiah 49:15–16 (NIV)

"Can a mother forget the baby at her breast and have no compassion on the child she has borne? Though she may forget, I will not forget you! See, I have engraved you on the palms of my hands."

God will never forget you. You are permanently written into His heart.

Living It Out

- o   **Acknowledge how you feel.**
  It's okay to admit when you feel invisible. Naming your feelings helps you bring them into the light so God can begin to heal them.

- o   **Invite God into your loneliness.**
  Instead of hiding from Him when you feel left out or unwanted, talk to Him. Let Him comfort you. Ask Him to remind you of your value.

- o   **Look for ways to see others.**
  Sometimes the best way to feel seen is to help others feel seen. Reach out to someone who might also feel left out. One small act of kindness can make a big difference.

- o   **Anchor your worth in God's truth.**
  The world is inconsistent—but God's love is constant. Your identity is rooted in Him, not in the approval of others.

Journal Prompt

- o   When was a time I felt invisible? How did I respond?

- o   What do I want God to remind me of when I feel overlooked?

- o   Who in my life might need to feel seen, and how can I show them love this week?

- o   What does it mean to me that God is El Roi, the God who sees me?

This Week's Challenge

This week, find one person who might be feeling unseen, and reach out. It could be someone sitting alone at lunch, a classmate who seems quiet, or even a friend who's been distant lately. Send a kind message, offer a compliment, or simply be present. When you reflect God's love to others, it fills something in your own heart too.

Dear God,

Sometimes I feel invisible—like no one sees me, hears me, or understands me. It hurts when I'm left out or feel forgotten. But I'm holding onto this truth: You see me. You know my heart, my thoughts, and every tear I've cried. You're not distant. You're right here with me.

Remind me that I am never alone. Even when I feel unnoticed by others, I am noticed by You. Help me see myself through Your eyes—loved, known, and valuable. Fill the lonely places in my heart with Your presence. And help me to see others the way You see them too.

Thank You for being El Roi—the God who sees me.

In Jesus' name,
Amen.

## Chapter 21

Emotions Are Messengers, Not Masters

What the Bible says about feelings and emotional intelligence

Let's Talk About It

One minute you're laughing with your friends, and the next—bam!—you're spiraling because someone left you on read. Or maybe your chest feels heavy for no clear reason. Or you're angry at the world, but can't explain why.

Welcome to the wild ride of being human.

Your emotions? They're not random. They're not weaknesses. They're not meant to be bottled up or boss you around. They're *messengers*—important signals that tell you something about what's going on inside of you. But they make terrible masters.

God created you with emotions on purpose—and He also gives you wisdom to handle them with grace, maturity, and freedom. That's called *emotional intelligence*—and yes, it's totally biblical.

Let's Break It Down: Emotions Aren't the Enemy

We often hear mixed messages:

- o   "Don't be so emotional."

- o   "Just follow your heart."

- o   "Ignore how you feel—it's not spiritual."

But the truth is, emotions themselves aren't wrong—they're just indicators. They tell you something is up.

Think of them like the dashboard lights in a car. When your "anger light" or "sadness light" flashes, it's a signal to pause and check under the hood—not drive off a cliff or yank out the wires.

Feel It, But Don't Follow It

Let's be clear: emotions are real, valid, and human. Even Jesus felt them!

- o   He wept at Lazarus' tomb. (John 11:35)
- o   He felt compassion for the hurting. (Matthew 9:36)
- o   He got righteously angry in the temple. (John 2:15)
- o   He sweat blood in deep anguish before the cross. (Luke 22:44)

But here's the thing—Jesus didn't let His emotions lead Him away from truth. He acknowledged them, brought them to God, and chose obedience through them. That's emotional intelligence in action.

What Is Emotional Intelligence?

Emotional intelligence is about understanding your feelings, managing them wisely, and relating to others with empathy. In other words:

- o   You *feel* your feelings
- o   You don't fake your feelings
- o   But you *don't follow* your feelings like they're always right

That's spiritual maturity. And it's powerful.

 Key Scriptures

Jeremiah 17:9 (NIV)

"The heart is deceitful above all things and beyond cure. Who can understand it?"

Let's be honest: our emotions sometimes lie. Fear can make you believe you're not safe, even when you are. Insecurity whispers you're not enough, even though God says you are. This verse reminds us: our feelings aren't always facts.

Instead of trusting every emotion blindly, we run them through God's truth.

"But the fruit of the Spirit is love, joy, peace, forbearance, kindness, goodness, faithfulness, gentleness and self-control."

Self-control isn't about stuffing feelings down. It's about responding instead of reacting. It's pausing before popping off in anger, praying before texting that guy, and choosing peace when chaos screams louder.

These fruits grow when we stay connected to the Spirit—He helps us handle our emotions with grace.

Proverbs 29:11 (NLT)

"Fools vent their anger, but the wise quietly hold it back."

This doesn't mean you can't be upset. But wisdom means knowing *how and when* to express those emotions in a way that honors God and respects others.

So yes—journal it out, talk to a trusted mentor, pray it through. Just don't let your emotions explode all over the place like a shaken soda can.

Practical Tools for Emotionally Intelligent Faith

Here's how to grow in your emotional awareness and wisdom:

- o **Name It to Tame It**
  Instead of saying "I'm fine" when you're not, try naming your emotion:

  "I feel anxious."

  "I feel rejected."

  "I feel confused."

  Bringing emotions into the light disarms their power.

o   **Pray It Out**

Your prayer life is not just for praise and requests—it's for emotional processing, too.

David, in the Psalms, poured it all out to God. Anger, fear, sorrow, hope—it's all in there.

You don't need perfect words. Just honest ones.

o   **Journal to Process, Not Just Vent**

Write about what happened, what you felt, and what God's Word says about it. This turns messy emotions into meaningful conversations with yourself and with God.

o   **Take Your Feelings to Scripture**

When you feel ___, go to ___:

Afraid → Psalm 56:3

Overwhelmed → Matthew 11:28

Insecure → Psalm 139

Angry → James 1:19–20

Sad → Revelation 21:4

Journal Prompt

o   What emotion do I struggle to express or admit? Why?

o   Have I ever followed a feeling that led me away from what God says? What happened?

o   How can I invite God into my emotions today?

 # This Week's Challenge

Pick one emotion that's been intense lately. Instead of ignoring or following it, do this:

- o   Name it.

- o   Pray about it.

- o   Find a verse that speaks truth into it.

- o   Write a short journal entry processing it.

 # Let's Pray

Dear God,

Thank You for creating me with emotions. Help me not to be afraid of my feelings—but also not ruled by them. Teach me to recognize what I'm feeling, bring it to You, and respond in a way that reflects Your heart. Grow the fruit of the Spirit in me—especially self-control, gentleness, and peace.

In Jesus name,
Amen.

## PART 3

RELATIONSHIPS
Faith in Real Life

Freindships, Family
and Loving Others

## Chapter 22

Real Friends, Real Drama

Okay, let's be real. Friendships can be amazing—like "laughing-so-hard-you-snort" kind of amazing. But they can also be... confusing, draining, or even a little toxic (ugh, middle school drama, anyone?). Whether you're the girl who has a million besties or the one who's still praying for her first real one, this chapter is for you.

Let's talk about the highs, the lows, and the in-betweens of friendship—and how to build relationships that are real, godly, and life-giving.

The Great Locker Room Meltdown

In 8th grade, I had what I call "The Great Locker Room Meltdown." Picture this: I walk into gym class, all sweaty and tired, and my "friend group" is huddled together whispering. One look and I knew they were talking *about me*. Ever been there?

I found out later one of them told the others that I was "too clingy" and "way too into church stuff." (Insert dramatic gasp here.) I wish I could say I handled it maturely, but I ugly cried into my hoodie and ghosted them all for a week.

But here's what I learned: not all friendships are meant to last. And that's okay. Some people come into your life for a season. Others? They're *forever friends*. But figuring that out takes wisdom, courage, and a whole lot of Jesus.

Navigating Toxic Friendships, Cliques, and Drama

Friendship drama is *real*. Cliques can make you feel left out, less-than, or like you need to *change who you are* just to fit in. Toxic friendships drain you—they leave you anxious, insecure, or always trying to prove yourself.

Here are a few *warning signs* of a toxic friendship:

- o   You feel like you're walking on eggshells around them.

- o   They make jokes that actually hurt.

- o   They only reach out when they need something.

- o   You feel worse about yourself after hanging out.

If you read that and thought of someone—deep breath. It doesn't mean you have to dump them with a dramatic text (please don't do that), but it may mean setting some healthy boundaries.

What It Means to Be a Godly Friend

Let's take a look at two beautiful verses:

Proverbs 17:17 (NIV):

"A friend loves at all times, and a brother is born for a time of adversity."

This verse reminds us that real friendship shows up even when things aren't fun or easy. A godly friend doesn't ditch you when you're going through stuff. She prays with you, listens, and stays.

John 15:13 (NIV):

"Greater love has no one than this: to lay down one's life for one's friends."

Jesus is the ultimate example of a friend. He loved us so much He gave His *life* for us. While we may not be called to literally die for our friends (praise!), we are called to show sacrificial love—listening, supporting, encouraging, forgiving. So ask yourself: "Am I being the kind of friend I want to have?"

Setting Boundaries & Choosing Wise Friends

God never asked you to be friends with *everyone*. That might sound weird at first, but hear me out—Jesus loved everyone, but He didn't hang out with *everyone*. He had His core group (the disciples), and even within that group, He was closest to a few (Peter, James, and John).

Here are some *friendship boundaries* that are totally okay (and actually super healthy):

- o   Saying "no" to gossip.

- o   Not feeling guilty for taking space.

- o   Choosing to walk away from drama.

- o   Guarding your heart (Proverbs 4:23, anyone?).

And when choosing friends, look for these qualities:

- o   Kindness and encouragement

- o   Honesty and trustworthiness

- o   Shared values and goals

- o   Joy! (Friendship should be fun, y'all!)

Journal Prompt

Take some quiet time this week and write about the following:

- o   What kind of friend do I want to be?

- o   Are there any friendships in my life that feel toxic or one-sided?

- o   Who are my "safe" people—those I feel loved, seen, and accepted by?

- o   What does Jesus teach me about friendship?

This Week's Challenge

Pray and ask God to show you which friendships in your life are helping you grow and which ones might need boundaries or even distance. Then, do this:

- o   Reach out to a friend who brings out the best in you. Let her know how much you appreciate her.
- o   Choose one way to be a better friend this week—maybe that's listening more, sending a kind note, or saying "sorry" first.

 # Let's Pray

Dear Heavenly Father,

Thank You for showing me what true friendship looks like. You love me unconditionally, and You never leave me—even when I'm at my worst. Help me to be a godly friend—kind, honest, forgiving, and loyal. Show me the friendships I need to hold onto and the ones I need to let go of. Give me courage to set boundaries, wisdom to choose wisely, and a heart that reflects Your love.

In Jesus name,
Amen.

You're never too young to choose friendships that are healthy, holy, and full of joy. Don't settle for drama when God has designed you for *deep, meaningful, Jesus-centered friendships.* You're worthy of love that lifts you higher—not weighs you down.

And if you're in a season where you feel friendless—don't panic. That's not your forever. Lean into Jesus. Ask Him for the right people. And in the meantime, be the kind of friend you're praying for.

You've got this, girl.

## Chapter 23

Toxic or One-Sided Friendships

When friendships hurt more than help
Building healthy, mutual connections

Let's talk about friendship—the kind that's supposed to bring laughter, comfort, and someone to split fries with at lunch. But what happens when it doesn't? What do you do when a friendship that *should* be life-giving starts to feel draining, confusing, or downright painful?

Maybe you've been there:
You're always the one reaching out.
You apologize when you didn't do anything wrong.
Your "friend" constantly puts you down or makes you feel small.
Or you give, and give, and give... and get crumbs in return.

Friendships can get complicated. But let's be honest: some relationships are just plain toxic. And even though it's hard to admit, not every friendship is meant to last forever.

If your heart hurts more than it heals around someone, it might be time to reevaluate whether that friendship is healthy.

God's Truth

God designed friendship to be a blessing, not a burden. Real friendship isn't about competition, manipulation, or emotional exhaustion. It's about love, trust, and mutual care.

Proverbs 17:17 says,

"A friend loves at all times, and a brother is born for a time of adversity."
That means a *true friend* sticks with you through the highs and lows—not

just when it's easy or fun.

Jesus also modeled what real friendship looks like. In **John 15:13**, He said,

"Greater love has no one than this: to lay down one's life for one's friends."
He showed us that healthy relationships are marked by selfless love—not
selfish gain.

And guess what? Nowhere in Scripture are we told to stay in relationships
that are toxic, manipulative, or emotionally harmful. In fact, **Proverbs 13:20**
gives us a warning:

"Walk with the wise and become wise, for a companion of fools suffers harm."
In other words, who you surround yourself with matters. It shapes who
you're becoming.

It's okay to set boundaries. It's okay to walk away from unhealthy friendships.
And it's more than okay to seek connections that are life-giving, mutual,
and rooted in love.

 Key Scriptures

Proverbs 17:17 (NIV)

"A friend loves at all times, and a brother is born for a time of adversity."

Real friends stick with you through hard times—not just when it's convenient.

John 15:13 (NIV)

"Greater love has no one than this: to lay down one's life for one's friends."

Healthy friendships are built on love and sacrifice, not selfishness.

Proverbs 13:20 (NIV)

"Walk with the wise and become wise, for a companion of fools suffers harm."

The people you hang around with will influence the direction of your life.

Living It Out

- o   **Recognize the red flags.**
  Toxic friendships often leave you feeling worse, not better. If you're constantly walking on eggshells, feeling used, or left out on purpose, pay attention to those warning signs.

- o   **Give yourself permission to let go.**
  Ending a friendship can feel scary, but holding on to something unhealthy just because it's familiar will keep you stuck. You are allowed to create space for better things.

- o   **Set healthy boundaries.**
  Not every difficult relationship has to end completely—but it's okay to limit how much time and energy you give. Boundaries aren't mean—they're wise.

- o   **4. Pursue mutual friendships.**
  Healthy friendships feel like a two-way street. Look for people who encourage you, listen to you, and make you feel safe to be your full, God-created self.

- o   **Trust God to fill the gaps.**
  Sometimes when we let go of the wrong people, it opens the door for the right ones. Ask God to bring friendships into your life that reflect His heart for you.

Journal Prompt

- o   How do I feel after spending time with certain friends? Do I feel built up or torn down?

- o   Have I ignored any red flags in my friendships lately? Why?

- o   What kind of friend do I want to be to others?

- o   What boundaries do I need to set to protect my emotional and spiritual health?

This Week's Challenge

Take an honest inventory of your closest friendships this week.
Ask yourself: Is this friendship helping me grow in the right direction? Does it honor God? Is it mutual? If something feels off, bring it to God in prayer and consider whether it's time to set a boundary—or possibly walk away.

And don't forget—you get to be that safe, kind, trustworthy friend to someone else too.

Let's Pray

Dear God,

Friendships can be beautiful, but sometimes they're hard and even hurtful. I don't always know how to navigate it all. Please give me wisdom to see clearly which relationships are healthy and which ones are not. Help me to recognize red flags and have the courage to step away when needed.

Fill my heart with Your love so that I don't cling to people who make me feel small or unworthy. Bring the right friends into my life—ones who love You and love me well. Teach me to be a true, loyal, and kind friend to others too.

Thank You for always being my faithful friend—even when everyone else fades away.

In Jesus' name,
Amen.

## Chapter 24

People-Pleasing & Boundaries

Ever feel like you can't catch a break because you're always trying to make everyone happy? Whether it's a friend, a teacher, a parent, or even a random person on social media, it can feel like your value depends on how many people approve of you. Maybe you say "yes" to things you don't want to do, change yourself to fit in, or constantly worry about what others think. It's exhausting, right?

People-pleasing isn't just about making nice with others—it's about craving their approval so much that you lose sight of who you really are and what God has called you to do. It's like trying to fill a cup with water when there's a hole in the bottom. No matter how hard you try, it never feels enough.

But here's the good news: God's approval is the only one that truly matters. You were created to live for Him, not to gain likes or popularity.

God's Truth

God doesn't call you to please people—He calls you to please Him. That might sound simple, but it's life-changing. When you live for God's approval, you get a freedom that the world can't give. You don't have to be a chameleon, shifting to match whatever crowd you're in. Instead, you can stand firm in who you are in Christ—someone already deeply loved and accepted.

In Galatians 1:10, Paul writes, *"Am I now trying to win the approval of human beings, or of God? Or am I trying to please people? If I were still trying to please people, I would not be a servant of Christ."* This verse is like a gut check. You can't serve both God and people's opinions. When you choose to live for God's approval, it's freeing, because you're not at the mercy of what others think.

Even Jesus didn't win everyone's approval. He wasn't trying to make every-one happy—and that didn't stop Him from walking in truth and living out His purpose.

In **John 2:24–25**, it says: *"But Jesus would not entrust himself to them, for he knew all people. He did not need human testimony about them, for he knew what was in each person."* Jesus wasn't swayed by human opinions because He knew His mission, and He knew His identity.

You're not here to meet other people's expectations. You're here to live for God's. And when you do that, the people who are meant to be in your life will love and appreciate you for who you really are.

What's Really Going On?

Let's look at a few truths that help untangle the pressure:

- o **Helping isn't the same as saving.**

  It's okay to support your friend, offer wisdom, and pray with them. But it's not your job to solve their life. God didn't ask you to carry burdens that only He can lift.

  Sometimes, when we try to fix everything, we unintentionally put ourselves in the place of God. Oof. That's not what we want, right? The most powerful thing you can do for someone might not be "fixing it," but pointing them to the One who can.

- o **Boundaries are not selfish—they're wise.**

  Even Jesus took time away from crowds to rest and be alone with the Father. If He needed boundaries, trust me—you do too. You're allowed to say:

  "I care about you, but I don't have the emotional space for this conversation right now."

  "I'm praying for you, but I'm not the best person to help with this."

  "I love you, but I need to take a step back."

  Real friends respect that. And the people who don't? That's a sign in itself.

o   **You can still love people while letting go.**

Sometimes, stepping back is the most loving thing you can do. It gives God room to work, and it frees you to rest in peace, not pressure. It also reminds the people around you that their healing doesn't depend on you—it depends on Jesus.

 Key Scriptures

Proverbs 4:23 (NIV)

"Above all else, guard your heart, for everything you do flows from it."

This isn't just about crushes—it's about your *emotional, mental, and spiritual well-being*. When you overextend yourself trying to fix everyone, your heart becomes overwhelmed, anxious, and heavy. Guarding your heart means knowing your limits, saying no sometimes, and making space for God to replenish you.

Galatians 6:2 (NIV)

"Carry each other's burdens, and in this way you will fulfill the law of Christ."

Yes—God wants us to be there for one another. But even this verse says burdens, not backpacks full of everyone's unresolved trauma. Helping doesn't mean *owning*. You can walk with someone, but you don't have to carry them the whole way.

Galatians 1:10 (NIV):
"Am I now trying to win the approval of human beings, or of God? Or am I trying to please people? If I were still trying to please people, I would not be a servant of Christ."

This verse is a reminder that trying to please people is not only exhausting—it's impossible to fully do while also living for God. Your identity and mission are found in His approval, not the world's.

John 2:24–25 (NIV):
"But Jesus would not entrust himself to them, for he knew all people. He did not need human testimony about them, for he knew what was in each person."

Even Jesus didn't waste His energy trying to win the approval of others. He lived with a clear purpose, knowing that what truly mattered was God's mission for Him.

Proverbs 29:25 (NIV):

"The fear of man will prove to be a snare, but whoever trusts in the Lord is kept safe."

 Fearing others' opinions traps you. But trusting in God's plan for you brings peace and safety. When you trust in God, you don't need to be afraid of rejection or criticism from others.

Living It Out

o **Know your worth in Christ:** The more you understand that God created you for a unique purpose, the less you'll care about fitting in with the crowd. You're already enough because of who you are in Him.

o **Set boundaries:** People-pleasing often comes from not setting healthy boundaries. Practice saying "no" when you need to, even if it's uncomfortable. You don't have to make everyone happy to be loved.

o **Let go of perfectionism:** Perfectionism often comes from the desire to be liked or approved. Remember, you don't have to be perfect to be loved. You don't have to have it all together to walk in your purpose.

o **Find your audience of One:** Jesus didn't care about everyone's opinion. He only cared about doing the will of His Father. The same goes for you—keep your focus on God, not on the crowd.

Real Talk: Signs You Might Be Taking on Too Much

o You're constantly anxious about your friends' problems

o You feel guilty for not responding immediately

o You're emotionally drained after every conversation

o You don't feel like you anymore—just a lifeline for others

If this is you, it's time to check in with God and ask:
Am I trying to do more than I was created to do?

What You Can Say Instead

- o "That sounds really heavy—have you talked to an adult or counselor about it?"

- o "I care about you, and I'm here to support you. But I also need some space to recharge."

- o "Let's pray together. God knows exactly what you need."

 Journal Prompt

- o What situations or people make me feel like I have to "fix" everything?

- o What boundaries might I need to set in my life right now?

- o What would it look like to trust God with the people I care about?

This Week's Challenge

Pick one situation or relationship where you feel emotionally drained. This week, pray over it and ask God to show you:

- o What is yours to carry?

- o What needs to be handed over to Him?

Then, practice setting one small boundary. (It could be as simple as not replying to messages late at night.)

Let's Pray

Dear God,

Sometimes I try to do too much. I want to help everyone, but I forget that You're the one who saves, not me. Teach me how to set healthy boundaries, love others well without burning out, and trust You with the people I care about. Remind me that stepping back doesn't mean giving up—it means giving it over to You.

In Jesus name,
Amen.

## Chapter 25

Peer Pressure to Fit In

Let's just be real for a second.

You know that moment when you're walking into a room and suddenly you're hyper-aware of everything—your clothes, your hair, what people are whispering, and whether you're about to sit at the "right" table?

Yeah. That.

Fitting in feels like the goal sometimes. You don't want to be weird. You don't want to be left out. You definitely don't want to be the girl who says "no" when everyone else is saying "yes."

But deep down, maybe you also don't want to lose yourself in the process of trying to belong.

Fitting In or Standing Out?

There was this girl I knew—we'll call her "Maya."

Maya was quirky in the best way. She wore socks with donuts on them, loved Jesus openly, and snorted when she laughed (adorably, I might add). But when she got to high school, everything changed.

Suddenly, the donut socks disappeared. The Bible verse in her bio got deleted. She stopped snorting when she laughed, and when someone brought up faith, she just stayed quiet.

One day I asked her, "Hey, why aren't you yourself anymore?"

And she shrugged and said, "I just didn't want to be *that girl*. You know? The one people think is too much or too different."

I've never forgotten that. Because *we've all been Maya.*

We've all felt the pressure to shrink, hide, or blend in just to be accepted. But let me tell you something that I wish Maya had believed:

You weren't created to blend in. You were made to *shine*.

Jesus Didn't Fit In Either

Jesus *totally* understands what it feels like to not fit in. In fact, He was constantly doing things that confused people, challenged social norms, and upset the "cool" crowd.

Key Verse – Romans 12:2 (NIV):

"Do not conform to the pattern of this world, but be transformed by the renewing of your mind. Then you will be able to test and approve what God's will is—His good, pleasing and perfect will."

Let's unpack that:

- o   "Do not conform" means don't squeeze yourself into a mold that was never made for you.

- o   "Be transformed" is about letting God shape your heart and mind so you can live boldly and authentically.

- o   And that last part? It means when you walk closely with God, you'll know who you are, what you're about, and how to live with confidence.

Jesus didn't conform, and because of that, He changed the world. You don't have to either. And trust me—you were made to make a difference, not just to *blend in.*

What Helps You Overcome the Pressure

Let's be honest: Resisting peer pressure is tough.

But here's what helps:

o	**Know Who You Are (and Whose You Are)**

The more you understand your identity in Christ, the less tempted you'll be to build your identity on likes, follows, or what your friend group thinks.

Here's just a glimpse of who God says you are:

Chosen (1 Peter 2:9)

Deeply loved (Romans 8:38-39)

Beautifully made (Psalm 139:14)

Called with purpose (Jeremiah 29:11)

Strong and courageous (Joshua 1:9)

o	**Surround Yourself with Real Ones**

Friends who let you be you are a gift. If someone makes you feel like you have to be less of yourself to be accepted… sis, that's not friendship. That's performance.

Find people who celebrate your faith, your weirdness, your goals, and your God-given sparkle.

o	**Ask God for Strength**

You're not meant to do this alone. Seriously—lean on God. Talk to Him when you're tempted to give in, and let Him remind you of your worth. He never runs out of patience. Or power.

Journal Prompt

Grab a notebook and reflect honestly on this:

o	Where in your life do you feel the pressure to fit in?

o	Are there places where you're hiding parts of who you really are?

o	What would it look like to stand out with courage and faith instead?

Take your time. This isn't about being perfect—it's about being real.

 # This Week's Challenge

Write a list called *"Who God Says I Am."*

Look up scriptures and make it personal. Here are some to get you started:

- o   "I am loved." **(John 3:16)**

- o   "I am a child of God." **(Galatians 3:26)**

- o   "I am forgiven." **(1 John 1:9)**

- o   "I am strong." **(Philippians 4:13)**

- o   "I am enough, because God is enough." **(2 Corinthians 12:9)**

Stick it on your mirror. Read it when you feel the pressure. Speak it over yourself every morning if you need to.

 # Let's Pray

Dear God,

Sometimes I feel like I have to change who I am to be liked, to be noticed, or to be accepted. Help me remember that I was created on purpose, for a purpose. Give me strength to stand out with confidence, even when it's hard. Teach me to love who You've made me to be. Help me say no when I need to, and to shine for You in every space I enter.

In Jesus' name,
Amen.

You don't need to blend in to belong.
You already belong—to the God who handcrafted you with love, strength, and a sparkle that can't be dimmed.

So shine, girl. Stand out. And let the world see Jesus through your beautiful, bold, one-of-a-kind life. You've got this.

## Chapter 26

The Fear of Rejection

Let's talk about something we all wish we could dodge forever: **rejection.**

Whether it's not getting invited, someone talking behind your back, being left on read, or just feeling like people are silently judging every move you make—it *hurts*.

And let's be real. It doesn't matter how confident you are, rejection can still make your heart feel like it's doing cartwheels on a trampoline.

But guess what? You can be **brave anyway.**
Not because you'll never be rejected. (Sorry, can't promise that.)
But because **your worth isn't on the line.**

That Time I Felt Totally Left Out

Okay, so once I showed up to school wearing this outfit I thought was super cute—denim overalls, neon scrunchie, and a tie-dye tee that said "Peace, Love, Tacos." (I still stand by the message.)

Anyway, I walk into the cafeteria, and I instantly feel it.

The stares. The whispering.

And one girl (let's call her "Brianna") actually pointed at my outfit and laughed out loud. Like, full-on gigglesnort.

I wanted the floor to open up and swallow me whole. I sat down, suddenly very aware that I was not "on trend," not cool, and definitely not invited to the table with the pretty Instagram girls.

For the rest of the day, I kept wondering:
"What's wrong with me?"
"Why don't they like me?"
"Should I change who I am?"

But that moment taught me something that's stuck with me since:
Rejection doesn't define you. God does.

Even Jesus Got Rejected

Yup, *even Jesus*.

The most loving, perfect, miracle-working Son of God was rejected,
mocked, betrayed, and misunderstood. By crowds. By religious leaders.
Even by His closest friends.

Key Verse – **Hebrews 13:6 (NIV):**

"The Lord is my helper; I will not be afraid. What can mere mortals do to me?"

In other words:

- o   People's opinions can be loud, but they don't get the final say.

- o   God stands with you, even when others don't.

- o   You can be brave—not because everyone approves of you, but because
  He does.

Jesus didn't let rejection stop Him from His purpose. And neither should you.

How to Overcome the Fear of Judgment

Let's break it down. Here's how to live bold when you feel like shrinking back:

- o   **Remember Who's Opinion Matters Most**

  God's opinion of you = **Unchanging. Loving. True.**
  He's not scrolling your feed looking for perfection. He sees your
  heart and delights in who you are. When you live for His "well
  done" instead of the world's "thumbs up," you walk in freedom.

o   **Affirm Yourself With Truth**

Instead of saying, "They didn't like me," try:

"I am accepted by God." **(Romans 15:7)**

"I am God's masterpiece." **(Ephesians 2:10)**

"I am chosen and not forsaken." **(1 Peter 2:9)**

These aren't just nice thoughts—they're real, powerful, identity-anchoring truths. Tape them to your mirror. Speak them over yourself. Let them drown out the lies.

o   **Rejection Doesn't Mean You're Wrong**

Sometimes being left out or judged doesn't mean you did anything wrong—it just means you're different. And different is not a bad thing.

In fact, it usually means you're *growing, shining, or standing for something* others don't understand yet.

Stay kind. Stay true. Stay standing.

Journal Prompt

Write this at the top of a blank page:
"What fear has been holding me back lately?"
Then let it out.

Is it the fear of what others think? Fear of failing? Fear of being laughed at? Get honest with God (and yourself), and ask: *What would I do if I wasn't afraid of being judged?*

Bravery starts with truth.

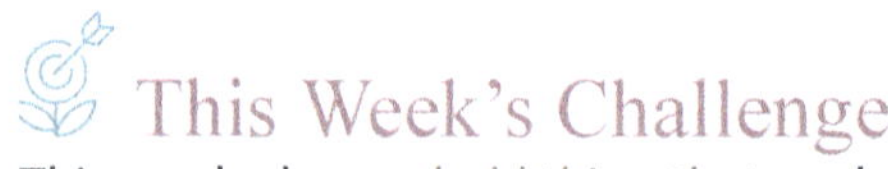

This Week's Challenge

This week, do *one bold thing that* you've been too scared to do—*even if your voice shakes.*

Here are some ideas:

- o   Wear the outfit you love, even if it's "different"

- o   Speak up for someone who's being left out

- o   Post something meaningful (even if no one double-taps)

- o   Say "no" to something that doesn't align with your values

- o   Pray out loud, even if your hands get sweaty

Small bravery still counts. The point is: *Do it scared. Do it anyway.*

 ## Let's Pray

Dear God,

Sometimes I care too much about what people think. I get scared of being judged or rejected, and I start shrinking instead of shining. But You remind me that I don't have to live for the approval of others—I already have Yours. Help me to be bold. Help me to speak, love, live, and dress like the person You created me to be. Even if others don't get it, give me peace and confidence in You.

In Jesus' name,
Amen.

So let me tell you one more time, in case no one else has lately:

- o   You are brave enough.

- o   You are not too much.

- o   You don't need to change who you are to be loved or accepted.

Rejection doesn't get the last word. God does.
And His word says: *You're chosen. You're called. You are enough.*

So go out there, and shine with courage.
Even if your hands shake. Even if your heart races.
You're not alone—God's with you, and that's all the approval you'll ever need.

## Chapter 27

When You Feel Left Out

Feeling Invisible? God Sees You.

Let's be honest.

There's no worse feeling than standing in a room full of people and still feeling... *alone.*

It could be something small—like not getting tagged in the group photo. Or something big—like walking past your friends at school and realizing they've made plans without you. Again.

You smile. Pretend it's fine. Act like it doesn't bother you. But deep down?

It hurts.

You start wondering:

- o   Did I do something wrong?

- o   Why didn't they include me?

- o   Am I just forgettable?

I've been there. More times than I care to admit.

The Cafeteria Moment I'll Never Forget

I still remember this moment from eighth grade.

I was walking into the cafeteria, tray in hand, searching for my people. I spotted the table where I usually sat—and then I saw it. *The empty seat that wasn't empty anymore.* Someone new had slid into my spot. No one looked up. No one waved me over.

So I kept walking. Right past them. Straight to the bathroom. I locked the stall and sat on the toilet seat (lid closed, don't worry), and cried.

Not because I didn't have other places to go. But because in that moment, it felt like no one saw me.
Like I didn't matter.
Like I was invisible.

But I Wasn't Invisible to God

In that lonely stall, I whispered a tiny prayer.
"God... do You see me?"

And though I didn't hear an audible answer, I felt it.
Deep in my spirit, a whisper rose up:
"Yes. I see you. You are never alone."

That moment changed everything.

Because here's what I've learned since then:
God *always* sees you.
Even when others don't.
Even when it feels like everyone else has a place and you're on the outside looking in.

Even when the world makes you feel small or forgotten—God never forgets you.

God Sees the Overlooked

You're not the first person to feel left out.

In fact, the Bible is filled with stories of people who were *overlooked, undervalued, or left behind*—and yet God used them in powerful ways.

Hagar was a servant girl who felt abandoned and alone in the desert. But in Genesis 16:13, she called God *"El Roi"—the God who sees me.*

David was the youngest of his brothers. When the prophet Samuel came to anoint the next king, no one even thought to call David in from the fields. But God saw him. Chose him. Raised him up.

"People look at the outward appearance, but the Lord looks at the heart."
—1 Samuel 16:7

Jesus Himself was rejected by many. Misunderstood. Mocked. And yet—He was never shaken by it. Why? Because He was rooted in *who He was, not in who accepted Him.*

 ## Key Scriptures

Here are a few verses I go back to when I'm feeling left out, lonely, or invisible:

Psalm 139:1-2
"You have searched me, Lord, and you know me... you perceive my thoughts from afar."

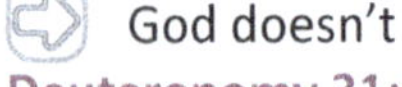 God doesn't just see your face. He sees your heart.

Deuteronomy 31:6
"Be strong and courageous... the Lord your God goes with you; he will never leave you nor forsake you."

Even if people walk away, God never will.

Isaiah 49:16
"See, I have engraved you on the palms of my hands."

Girl, your name is literally written on God's hand. That's how known and loved you are.

Real Talk: Not Everyone Will Get You— And That's Okay

Let me just say this: not being invited doesn't mean you're unworthy.
Not getting the text doesn't mean you're unwanted.
Not being included doesn't mean you're not incredible.

Some people will overlook you because you're different.
Others may be wrapped up in their own stuff and just forget.
Either way—it says more about them than it does about you.

And sometimes... God allows certain doors to close because He's protecting you or preparing you for something better.
Yes, even in friendships.

 Journal Prompt

Grab your journal (or Notes app) and write this at the top:
"God Sees Me Even When..."

Then fill it in.
Be honest. Be raw. Let it out.

- o   God sees me even when I sit alone at lunch.

- o   God sees me even when the texts stop coming.

- o   God sees me even when I don't feel pretty, smart, or wanted.

- o   God sees me even when I feel like I'm too much—or not enough.

Let your soul breathe. And then remind yourself:

"I am not invisible. I am seen, chosen, and loved—by the One who matters most."

Let's Pray

Dear Heavenly Father,

,

Sometimes I feel so left out. So unseen.
But Your Word says You never forget me.
You know my name. You see my heart.
Even when others don't include me, help me remember that I belong to You.
Wrap me up in Your love and remind me I'm never alone.

In Jesus name,
Amen.

## Chapter 28

Loneliness & Not Belonging

Loneliness is one of the hardest emotions to deal with, especially when you feel like you don't belong. Maybe you're the new kid in school, or perhaps you feel like you just don't fit in with your friends. The world often tells you that if you're different or don't follow the crowd, you're on your own. It feels like everyone else has their group, their place, their people—and you're just watching from the outside. Maybe you scroll through social media and see groups of friends laughing, having fun, living life to the fullest, and you wonder, Why doesn't that ever include me? Or maybe you're trying to connect but still feel distant, like there's an invisible wall between you and everyone else.

Loneliness can make you feel like you're the only one who doesn't belong. But the truth is, loneliness doesn't have to define you. God has made you for community. Your identity is rooted in His family, and no matter how lonely you may feel in a moment, He promises you are never truly alone.

God's Truth

God's Word speaks directly to our feelings of loneliness and not belonging. It's easy to believe that if you're different, you're alone. But God says *you are never alone.* **Deuteronomy 31:6** promises that God is with you wherever you go, and He will never leave or forsake you. You don't have to face life by yourself.

In **Romans 8:15–17**, it says: *"The Spirit you received does not make you slaves, so that you live in fear again; rather, the Spirit you received brought about your adoption to sonship. And by him we cry, 'Abba, Father.' The Spirit himself testifies with our spirit that we are God's children. Now if we are children, then we are heirs—heirs of God and co-heirs with Christ."*

This verse reminds us that as a follower of Christ, you are a part of God's family. You are not alone; you belong. You are an heir to God's promises, and you have been adopted into His family. No matter what happens here on earth, you have a forever place in His Kingdom.

You were created for connection—with God first, and with others who love and encourage you in Him. In 1 Corinthians 12:27, Paul reminds us that, as believers, we are the body of Christ. *"Now you are the body of Christ, and each one of you is a part of it."* This means that you are never isolated. Even when you feel like you don't fit in with the world around you, you belong to the larger family of believers.

 Key Scriptures

Deuteronomy 31:6 (NIV):
"Be strong and courageous. Do not be afraid or terrified because of them, for the Lord your God goes with you; he will never leave you nor forsake you."

This promise reminds you that no matter how alone you may feel, God is always by your side. You're never truly alone.

Romans 8:15–17 (NIV):
"The Spirit you received brought about your adoption to sonship. And by him we cry, 'Abba, Father.' The Spirit himself testifies with our spirit that we are God's children. Now if we are children, then we are heirs—heirs of God and co-heirs with Christ."

You belong in God's family. You are not alone; you have a Father who loves you and calls you His own.

1 Corinthians 12:27 (NIV):
"Now you are the body of Christ, and each one of you is a part of it."

God has made you a part of something bigger than yourself. You belong to the family of believers, the body of Christ, and no one is an outsider in God's eyes.

Living It Out

o   **Know that God is with you:** No matter how lonely you may feel, God's presence is always with you. Remember that He will never leave you or forsake you. Speak to Him whenever you feel isolated—He listens and cares about your heart.

o   **Find your community:** God made you for relationship and connection. Seek out other believers, whether in a youth group, a church community, or a group of friends who share your faith. You belong in His family, and there are others who are also seeking true connection.

o   **Embrace your unique place:** You don't have to be like everyone else. Even if you feel different or out of place, God has a purpose for you in His Kingdom. Your uniqueness is a gift to His family, and you play a vital role in the body of Christ.

o   **Reach out to others:** Sometimes, the best way to fight loneliness is by showing love to others. Reach out to someone who may also be feeling disconnected or isolated. When you serve others, you experience the connection and community you're longing for.

This Week's Challenge

This week, whenever you feel alone, take a moment to remember that you belong to God's family. Write a list of people you can turn to for support and community, whether it's your youth group, a friend from church, or your family.

If you don't have a community like this, ask God to bring people into your life who will encourage you in your faith.

When you feel lonely, remind yourself of this truth: You are never truly alone. God is always with you, and you belong to Him.

Let's Pray

Dear Heavenly Father,

Thank You for always being with me, even when I feel alone. I admit that there are times when loneliness creeps in, and I start to feel disconnected from the world around me. But I know that I am never truly alone. You have promised to be with me always, and I belong to Your family. Help me to remember that truth when I feel isolated, and remind me that my identity is secure in You. Bring people into my life who will encourage me and help me grow in my faith. Thank You for making me a part of Your family and for always being near. I love You.

In Jesus' name,
Amen.

## Chapter 29

The Comparison Game

Why Measuring Up Isn't the Same as Standing Strong

I once knew a girl named Lila. Bright, creative, kind-hearted—but she couldn't see it. Every day, she'd compare herself to her best friend, Zoe. Zoe was outgoing, athletic, had tons of followers, and seemed to shine in every room she walked into.

Lila felt... invisible.

Even when people complimented her, she'd brush it off, believing she'd never measure up. One day, after yet another spiral of overthinking, she opened her Bible and stumbled across that verse in **2 Corinthians**. Something clicked.

What if *every* thought wasn't *truth*? What if she could choose what stayed and what had to go?

That was the beginning of her comeback. Let's just be honest for a second.

Scrolling Instagram can feel like an emotional rollercoaster. One minute you're watching your friend's hilarious dance fail, and the next you're deep in someone else's perfect vacation photos, wishing you had her hair, her skin, her confidence, her boyfriend, her life. (And maybe her dog too... because *seriously, even the dog is cuter than me?!)*

Comparison is sneaky. It shows up when you least expect it. At school, at youth group, even at Target. (How does *everyone* look good at Target except me?)

But here's the truth: comparison is a thief. It steals your joy, your peace, your confidence, and your sense of who God made you to be.

And the worst part? We often do it without even realizing.

When You Start Feeling Less Than

I'll never forget the day I sat in math class and watched a girl across the room get complimented by literally everyone—for her hair, her outfit, even the way she wrote her notes. Like, seriously? Her handwriting is cute too?

And there I was, sitting in the back row with frizzy bangs, a stain on my hoodie (from a rogue pizza roll), and the world's worst attempt at eyeliner. I felt invisible. And then I felt dumb for feeling invisible.

I went home that day and tried to "fix" everything. I redid my hair. Changed my outfit twice. Rewatched makeup tutorials. I even practiced handwriting, like somehow prettier cursive would make me a better person.

But the more I tried to "measure up," the worse I felt. Because the truth is—comparison will always leave you empty.

What the Bible Says About Comparison

Let's look at what God says:

"Each of you should test your own actions. Then you can take pride in yourself, without comparing yourself to someone else, for each one should carry their own load."
—Galatians 6:4–5 (NIV)

Paul is saying: *Hey, focus on your own lane.* You've got your own path, your own journey, your own God-given calling. Don't waste time comparing your behind-the-scenes to someone else's highlight reel.

Another one:

"I praise you because I am fearfully and wonderfully made; your works are wonderful, I know that full well."
—Psalm 139:14 (NIV)

Did you catch that? *Fearfully and wonderfully made.* That's you. God doesn't make copies. He makes masterpieces. He didn't mess up when He made you. He didn't forget something or run out of sparkle.

When we compare ourselves to others, we're basically telling God, "Hey, I think You should've made me like her instead." But God doesn't make mistakes. And He sure didn't start with you.

The Homecoming Meltdown

Let me tell you about Emma. She's gorgeous, hilarious, and the most down-to-earth girl ever—but for some reason, she always compared herself to other people.

At homecoming, she walked in looking stunning. Like, jaws-dropped stunning. But halfway through the night, I found her in the bathroom crying. Why? Because another girl wore the same dress... and somehow, Emma thought the other girl looked better.

She said, "I just feel like I'm never the girl. I'm always just... there."

Comparison had robbed her joy. It didn't matter how beautiful or loved she was—she couldn't see it through the lens of insecurity.

So I hugged her, handed her a tissue (or ten), and reminded her: *You're not meant to be anyone else's version of beautiful. You're already exactly who you were meant to be.*

We ended up laughing so hard that night that our mascara basically moved to our cheeks. It was worth it.

Journal Prompt

Take a few moments and sit with these questions. Be honest—it's just you and God here.

- o What do you find yourself comparing yourself to the most?

- o What lies do you believe when you start comparing?

- o What truths from God's Word can replace those lies?

Now finish this prayer sentence in your own words:

"God, when I compare myself to others, I feel _____. But You say I am _____."

This Week's Challenge

Here's your mission this week (don't worry, it's a good one):

Catch yourself comparing—and stop. Replace the thought.

Every time you catch yourself thinking "She's so much prettier/funnier/ smarter than me," flip the script and say:

"She's amazing. And I am too."

This isn't about pretending you don't struggle—it's about reminding yourself of truth in the middle of the struggle.

Bonus move? Compliment the girl you were comparing yourself to. Break the comparison cycle with kindness. It's *weirdly freeing.*

Let's Pray

Dear Heavenly Father,

Sometimes I get caught in the trap of comparison, and it steals the joy You've given me. I look around and think I don't measure up—but You see me differently. You call me beautiful, chosen, and loved. Help me to stop measuring my worth by someone else's life. Help me to believe that I am fearfully and wonderfully made. Teach me to celebrate others without doubting myself. Fill me with confidence that comes from knowing who I am in You.

In Jesus name,
Amen.

Comparison might feel normal, but it doesn't have to be your reality. You were never made to measure up to anyone else—you were made to reflect *God's image* in your own unique way.

Next chapter? We're talking about anxiety—and how to stop spiraling when life feels overwhelming.

Spoiler alert: You're stronger than your feelings, and God's peace is real.

## Chapter 30

Crushes, Dating & Guarding Your Heart

Let's be honest—crushes are a whole experience.

One second you're just living your life, eating your pizza, and then boom— your heart decides someone's smile is the most magical thing on planet Earth. Suddenly you're overthinking every text, re-reading "good morning" like it's a love letter, and asking your friends, *"Do you think he likes me??"*

You are not alone. Been there. Lived that.

Crushes are fun, exciting, awkward, and confusing. But they also open up some big questions like:

- o   Is it okay to like someone?

- o   What does God think about dating?

- o   How do I protect my heart and not totally lose my mind?

Let's talk about it.

That One Crush I Was Sure Was "The One"

Okay, so picture middle school me: braces, side bangs, and a hoodie that said "LOVE PINK" in letters the size of my confidence.

There was this guy—let's call him Ethan. He played guitar, wore Vans, and had that floppy haircut that made 12-year-old hearts flutter.

One day he asked to borrow a pencil in math class, and I was convinced this was a sign from the Lord. I wrote his name in bubble letters on my notebook. I even prayed, "God, if he's the one, let him pick me for the group project."

Spoiler alert: he didn't. And two weeks later, he was "talking" to my friend.

Cue heartbreak, dramatic playlist, and me dramatically staring out the bus window like I was in a music video.

Looking back, I realized something: I wasn't just crushing on a guy. I was crushing my own identity to try and feel seen, noticed, and chosen.

And that's not what God wants for your heart.

Truth Talk: God's Design for Love

Let's talk about what love really looks like—the kind God designed for us.

Proverbs 4:23 (NIV):

"Above all else, guard your heart, for everything you do flows from it."

Your heart is *precious*. It's the center of your thoughts, emotions, dreams, and identity. When we give too much of it away—too fast, too soon—we can end up feeling empty or confused.

God's design for love is beautiful. It's patient, pure, honest, and rooted in respect and commitment—not drama or confusion.

Here's the thing: *Dating isn't bad.* But it's not just a game or something to do because "everyone else is doing it." It's something worth being intentional about. Relationships are powerful—and they shape who you become.

So instead of asking, *"Can I date?"* try asking:
"Is this helping me grow closer to God—or pulling me away from Him?"

Boundaries: Not Just Rules, but Protection

Let's talk boundaries. And no, they're not just "churchy" rules to kill your vibe. Boundaries are like guardrails—they keep your heart safe when feelings get intense.

o   **Healthy emotional boundaries:**

Don't share your entire life story with someone you've known for two weeks.

Protect your thoughts and feelings. You don't have to overshare to be loved.

Make sure your self-worth isn't tied to someone else's opinion of you.

o   **Healthy physical boundaries:**

Honor your body. It's not just about "how far is too far?" but "how can I respect what God made?"

Talk to a trusted adult or mentor about what boundaries are right for you.

Know your values before you're in the moment. That's real wisdom.

You are not "too much" for wanting to be cherished.
You are not "lame" for choosing purity.
You are deeply valued—and anyone worthy of your heart should treat you like the daughter of the King that you are.

Journal Prompt

Write this in your journal:

"What do I want in a future relationship—and what does God want for me?"

Get honest. List what you hope for, what makes you feel safe, and what red flags you want to avoid. Then compare your list with what Scripture says about love (try reading 1 Corinthians 13:4–7). Is your list aligned with God's best?

This Week's Challenge

This week, take one intentional step to protect your heart. That might be:

o   Muting/unfollowing accounts that glorify toxic relationship stuff

o   Talking to a mentor about your boundaries

o   Pausing a texting situation that's taking over your brain o   Praying before you start catching feelings (yes, you can do that!)

Be proud of yourself for being intentional. That's not boring—it's bold.

 # Let's Pray

Dear God,

You know my heart—even the parts I try to hide. Sometimes I get caught up in crushes and wanting to be liked, and I forget that I'm already fully known and deeply loved by You. Help me to guard my heart, set healthy boundaries, and seek relationships that honor You. Show me what real love looks like, and help me to wait for Your best. When I feel lonely or insecure, remind me that You are enough.

In Jesus' name,
Amen.

You don't have to rush.
You don't have to settle.
You are worth waiting for.
You are already chosen.

So whether you're crushing, dating, or just chilling with snacks and Netflix—remember:

Love begins with knowing your worth in God.

And girl, He loves you more than any boy ever could.

## Chapter 31

Social Media & Your True Worth

Let's talk about the elephant in the room—or more like, the glowing rectangle in your hand. Social media. It's fun, right? You can keep up with your friends, find hilarious memes, watch cute puppy videos, and maybe even get inspired by someone's Bible verse post or aesthetic journaling page. But let's be honest—it also comes with *a lot* of pressure.

You open Instagram or TikTok and see someone with the perfect outfit, flawless skin, a dreamy friend group, and what looks like a way better life than yours. Suddenly, you go from feeling okay to feeling... less than. Your smile feels awkward. Your hair feels boring. Your life feels small. And before you know it, you're stuck in the comparison trap.

Social media isn't evil. But it becomes dangerous when we let it define our worth. Likes, followers, filters, and highlights can't show the whole picture. And they definitely can't show your *value*—because that comes from something way deeper than your feed.

God's Truth

Here's what God says: Your identity isn't found on a screen—it's found *in Him*. You were created in His image, not your favorite influencer's. You were called to run your race—not hers, not theirs, not the one trending on TikTok. And the beautiful, freeing truth? You're already enough without trying to edit your way into someone else's version of success.

You don't need to *keep up*—you need to *look up*. Fix your eyes on the One who knows you fully and loves you completely. Because your worth isn't based on attention—it's based on adoption. You're God's daughter. You belong. You have purpose. No amount of likes can touch that kind of value.

The Emotional Rollercoaster of Likes

Let me take you back to my 14-year-old self. I had just posted the perfect selfie. You know the kind—you take 47 versions of the same picture, finally find the one, slap on a filter, and post it with a "casual" caption like, "Just vibing."

And then... I waited.

10 likes.
20 likes.
Annnnd... it stalled.

Meanwhile, my friend posted a blurry pic of her cat sneezing and got 143 likes and three fire emojis.

Cue the spiral:
"Is something wrong with me?"
"Why didn't they like mine?"
"Maybe I should've edited it more... should I delete it??"

Y'all. It was one picture. But it felt like my self-worth was hanging on that like button.

Looking back, I realize something important: I let the internet decide my value. And it doesn't get to do that.
Not for me. Not for you.

What the Bible Says About True Worth

Social media might rank you based on numbers, but God doesn't.

Key Verse – 1 Samuel 16:7 (NIV):

"People look at the outward appearance, but the Lord looks at the heart."

Let's unpack that:

o   The world is obsessed with filters, edits, and perfect angles.

o   But God? He's looking at you. The real you.

o   Not the version of you with 10 filters and a perfectly posed caption. The *unfiltered, unedited, full-of-potential YOU.*

That means when you're comparing your behind-the-scenes to someone else's highlight reel, you're missing the bigger truth:

Your value has never been measured in likes.
God's love isn't based on your follower count.
You are already chosen, seen, and deeply loved—just as you are.

What Helps You Overcome the Comparison Game

Let's get real about what helps when social media starts messing with your mind.

o   **Remember What's Real**

Behind every perfect post is a person with real struggles, bad days, and messy emotions. No one's life is as flawless as their grid.

When you remember that Instagram isn't real life, it's easier to scroll with grace—and a little side-eye for that suspiciously perfect breakfast bowl.

Remember: Everyone is showing their highlight reel, not their behind-the-scenes. Don't compare your real life to their filtered one.

o   **Speak Truth Over Yourself**

Comparison steals joy. But truth? Truth sets you free.

Every time you catch yourself thinking, "I'm not enough," counter it with what God says:

"I praise You because I am fearfully and wonderfully made."
– Psalm 139:14

"You are altogether beautiful, my darling; there is no flaw in you."
– Song of Songs 4:7

"God chose me before the world began." **– Ephesians 1:4** (paraphrased)

o   **Control What You Consume**

If an account constantly makes you feel like you're not measuring up, its okay to **unfollow**. Protect your peace. You don't owe anyone access to your heart.

You are the gatekeeper of your feed. Make it one that builds you up, not breaks you down.

Set healthy boundaries with social media. Try taking a break or limiting your screen time, especially if it's messing with your joy.

Journal Prompt

Take a few minutes and write this down:

"What do I wish people knew about the real me?"

No filters. No edits. Just honesty.

Write about your passions, your heart, your struggles—what makes you you. Then ask: "Am I showing up that way in real life? Or am I trying to perform?"

Let this be a chance to reconnect with your authentic self—the one God loves completely.

This Week's Challenge

Take a one-day (or one-week) social media break. Or if that feels like too much, just start by unfollowing any account that:

o   Makes you feel less than

o   Triggers comparison or anxiety

o   Encourages a lifestyle that doesn't align with your values

Instead, follow people and pages that inspire your faith, creativity, and confidence.

Bonus: Use that time to read a chapter in the Bible, journal, or go outside and do something un-Instagrammable (but totally life-giving).

 # Let's Pray

Dear God,

Jesus, help me stop chasing approval in the scroll. I get so caught up in comparing myself to everyone else, and it leaves me feeling like I'll never be enough. But You say I already am—because I'm Yours. Remind me that my identity is safe in You, not in likes or filters or what everyone else is doing. Teach me to celebrate who I am, just as You made me, and to run my own race with joy. I want to fix my eyes on You—not the feed. Help me live free from comparison and full of confidence in who I am in You.

In Jesus name,
Amen.

You are more than your profile.
More than your selfies.
More than the number next to the heart icon.

You are deeply loved by a God who sees past every filter and still says, "You're amazing."

So live unfiltered.
Love deeply.
Scroll wisely.
And never forget your true worth.

Chapter 32:
Family Conflict & Misunderstandings

Let's just say it: family can be hard. Yes, they might be the ones who love us the most, but they're also the ones who know *exactly* how to push our buttons. Like, how does your little brother *always* manage to bother you at the *worst* time?

Or why does your mom ask if your room is clean when you're clearly in an emotional crisis?

We've all been there. This chapter is all about navigating those family feels—the good, the awkward, the frustrating—and learning how to honor your family, even when things get messy.

When You Don't Get Along With Your Parents or Siblings

Okay, story time.

There was a week when my mom and I argued every single day. Like clockwork. I would say something snarky, she'd raise an eyebrow (you know the eyebrow), and things would spiral into a dramatic "I just need to be alone!" moment, complete with bedroom door slams.

Looking back, I wasn't mad at my mom—I was overwhelmed with school, friendships, and feeling like she just didn't get me. Sound familiar?

Here's the thing: *disagreement is normal*. You're not a bad daughter or sister because you get annoyed or frustrated. But how you respond in those moments? That's where growth happens.

Sometimes we just need a minute to breathe. And other times, we need to sit down and have a real, honest convo—even if it feels awkward.

Honoring Your Family While Still Being Honest

Let's look at this verse:

Ephesians 6:1-2 (NIV)

"Children, obey your parents in the Lord, for this is right. 'Honor your father and mother'—which is the first commandment with a promise."

This doesn't mean you have to agree with every decision your parents make, or that your siblings will magically stop being annoying if you pray hard enough. (I tried. Doesn't work.)

Honoring your family means treating them with *respect*, even when you disagree. It means being honest about your feelings without slamming doors or throwing sarcasm like confetti.

You can say:

- o "I need some space to calm down first."

- o "I felt hurt when you said that. Can we talk about it?"

- o "I love you, but I don't agree, and I'd like to explain why."

Honesty + respect = honor.

Grace and Forgiveness at Home

Here's a not-so-fun truth: Your family is made up of imperfect people—just like you.

They're going to mess up. You're going to mess up. And that's why we all need a whole lot of grace.

Colossians 3:13 (NLT)

"Make allowance for each other's faults, and forgive anyone who offends you. Remember, the Lord forgave you, so you must forgive others."

Forgiveness doesn't mean pretending everything is fine. It means choosing not to hold on to the bitterness. It's saying, "I'm not going to let your mistake become a weight I carry forever."

When your sibling *borrows your stuff* without asking (AGAIN)… When your parent *misunderstands* your heart… When emotions explode and no one says sorry first…

Take a breath. Be the first to extend grace. Not because they deserve it, but because Jesus gave it to you.

Journal Prompt

Find a quiet spot and reflect on these:

- o   Who in my family do I struggle with the most—and why?

- o   How can I express my feelings in a way that's honest *and* honoring?

- o   Where do I need to give grace or forgive?

- o   What's one thing I actually love about my family (even if they drive me nuts sometimes)?

This Week's Challenge

Choose to be the *peacemaker* in your home this week. It doesn't mean avoiding conflict—it means *choosing calm over chaos.*

Try this:

- o   Compliment a family member (even if it feels weird at first).

- o   Do one thing around the house *without being asked.*

- o   Say "I'm sorry" first—even if it's just for how you responded.

Watch how even small acts of love shift the atmosphere.

Let's Pray

Dear God,

Thank You for my family—even when they frustrate me. You've placed me in this home for a reason. Help me to love them with patience and kindness. Give me the courage to be honest without being hurtful. Teach me to forgive quickly and offer grace like You do for me. Fill my heart with peace and remind me that You're working in my family, even when I can't see it.

In Jesus' name,
Amen.

Listen, family life isn't perfect—and it's not supposed to be. But God can use even the messy moments to shape us, teach us, and grow us in love.

You're not alone in the chaos. You're growing. You're learning. And through it all, you're becoming more like Jesus.

And hey—if your little brother still eats your snacks without asking? Offer him grace…and maybe hide the good snacks better next time.

Chapter 33:
Pause the Noise

Let's talk about noise.

Not just the kind that comes from your earbuds or the hallway at school. I'm talking about the other noise—the constant buzz of culture, opinions, alerts, pressure, likes, comments, comparisons, notifications, and expectations.

It's a lot.

There's this unspoken rule floating around, especially online, that says: *"If you're not constantly posting, constantly talking, constantly hustling— you're falling behind."*

But here's the truth:
Busyness doesn't make you better. Loudness doesn't make you stronger. And just because the world is shouting, doesn't mean you have to shout back.

The Day I Couldn't Hear Myself Think

I remember a day where I felt like I was drowning in everyone else's voices.

I had scrolled Instagram for over an hour (without meaning to). I had three text threads going, music blaring, and a to-do list longer than my leg. And yet, I felt... disconnected. From myself. From God. From peace.

I was filled, but not *full*.

That night, I turned off my phone and just sat still. For five minutes. No noise. No scrolling. Just... quiet.

It felt awkward at first, like I didn't know what to do with myself. But then something happened—my heart exhaled. Like it had been holding its breath all day.

And in that quiet, I heard God's whisper. Not out loud, but in that soft place deep down. The kind of whisper that says,
"I'm here. I see you. I've been waiting."

God's Invitation: Be Still

Psalm 46:10 says, "Be still and know that I am God."

Just... be still. Stillness is where the real magic happens. It's where your identity gets re-centered. Where your fears get quieted. Where your worth gets rewritten by *God's truth, not the world's noise.*

Let's Get Real

You're growing up in a generation where silence is rare.

If there's a pause, it gets filled with TikToks, Snapchats, texts, or Spotify playlists. And none of those things are bad—but when they become your constant background music, it's hard to hear what's happening inside you.

Let me ask you this:

- When's the last time you sat alone without your phone?

- Or read your Bible without rushing?

- Or journaled your actual thoughts—not just curated them for a post?

Those moments matter more than you know.

Truth You Can Hold Onto

Here's what I want you to hear:

- You don't need to earn God's attention.
- You don't need to post a verse to be spiritual.
- You don't need to prove anything. He's already listening.

The world will keep yelling, but God always whispers.
And whispers are only heard when we slow down enough to lean in.

Action Step: The 5-Minute Reset

Try this. Just for today.

Unplug.
No music. No scrolling. No alerts.
Find a quiet spot—your bed, your closet, the backyard.

Set a timer for five minutes.
Close your eyes.
Breathe in. Breathe out.
Talk to God. Or just sit with Him.
Let your heart speak.
Or write what you're feeling in a journal.
No filters. No edits. Just you.

Then do it again tomorrow.

A Whisper That Changes Everything

You might be surprised what happens in the quiet.
You'll start to hear things like:

- o "You're enough."
- o "You're seen."
- o "You're loved."
- o "You don't have to be like everyone else."

You'll realize the voice that matters most isn't in the comments or the likes
or the DMs. It's in the stillness. And it's *God's voice*, reminding you that you
are known, chosen, and deeply loved—not because you're busy or loud or
successful, but because you're His.

 ## Let's Pray

Dear Heavenly Father,

Help me to pause. Help me to unplug and be present with You. Teach me to be still—to hear Your voice above the noise. Quiet the chaos in my heart and remind me who I am. Thank You for meeting me in the silence.

In Jesus name, Amen.

LIVING Unshakable

Roadmap Built on Truth, Not Trends

<h1 style="text-align:center">Chapter 34:
Know Who You Are (and Whose You Are)</h1>

You've probably heard this one before: "Just be yourself!" Sounds great, right? But what if you're not quite sure who *yourself* is? What if one minute you feel like a confident, go-getter girl ready to take on the world, and the next you're overthinking everything you said in math class three days ago? (Been there. Math brain fog is real.)

Let's be real—culture LOVES to tell you who you *should* be. Instagram says you need a certain aesthetic. TikTok says you should have a 10-step skincare routine, drink green smoothies, and somehow wake up at 5 a.m. looking flawless. Even your friend group might unintentionally make you feel like you need to act a certain way to fit in. And slowly, without even realizing it, you start performing instead of living. Pretending instead of being.

But God? He flips the script.

God Says You're Already Enough

Here's what God says about you: *"You are a chosen people, a royal priesthood, a holy nation, God's special possession"* **(1 Peter 2:9)**. That means you don't have to earn His love, approval, or acceptance. You already have it. You were handcrafted by the Creator of the universe with intention and purpose. That's wild, right?

You're not just liked. You're loved. You're not just enough. You're chosen.

Let that sink in.

The Labels You Wear

I used to think my identity came from what I did or how people saw me.
I was "the smart girl," "the nice one," or sometimes, "the awkward one"
(middle school was a weird time, okay?). When someone complimented
me, I felt seen. When I got criticized, I felt crushed. It was like I handed
everyone around me a label maker and let them stick words on me.

But those labels don't define me. And they don't define you.

Only the One who made you gets to name you. And He calls you:

o   Loved (Romans 8:38-39)

o   His masterpiece (Ephesians 2:10)

o   More than a conqueror (Romans 8:37)

Finding Your True Identity

Knowing who you are begins with knowing Whose you are. When you start
from that place, everything changes. You'll begin to:

o   Stop striving to fit in and start standing firm in your faith.

o   Trade comparison for confidence.

o   Make decisions rooted in truth, not trends.

Journal Prompt

o   What labels have you believed about yourself that don't match
      what God says about you?

o   Which truth from Scripture do you want to hold onto this week?

This Week's Challenge

Write down 3 truths from Scripture about your identity and put them where you'll see them often—your mirror, your lock screen, or even in your journal. (Sticky notes = underrated spiritual tools.)

Pick one verse about your identity and memorize it this week. Repeat it to yourself when you're tempted to compare or doubt.

Let's Pray

Dear Heavenly Father,

Thank You for creating me with purpose and calling me Yours. Help me silence the lies and remember the truth: I am chosen, loved, and set apart. Teach me to see myself the way You see me and to walk in confidence knowing who I am in You.

In Jesus name,
Amen.

## Chapter 35

Guard Your Heart Without Hardening It

Don't just follow your heart—guide it wisely
Ask: Will this bring me closer to Jesus or pull me away?

Have you ever been told to *"follow your heart"*?
It sounds poetic. Inspiring, even. Like something you'd see on a Pinterest quote over a sunset.

But here's the thing—sometimes your heart doesn't know where it's going.

One minute it's chasing dreams. The next it's falling for someone who barely texts back. Sometimes your heart leads you into beautiful places, and sometimes...it leads you straight into heartbreak.

When someone lets you down, when a friendship fades, when you've poured everything into something that doesn't give anything back—you might feel tempted to shut your heart down altogether. *No one gets in. No one gets close. No one gets to hurt me again.*

But here's the truth: God never asked you to harden your heart.
He asks you to *guard it.*

There's a difference. One builds a wall; the other builds wisdom.

God's Truth

Proverbs 4:23 says:

"Above all else, guard your heart, for everything you do flows from it."

Your heart is precious. It's the core of your emotions, your dreams, your choices. And the Bible says it's worth guarding.Not because love is risky or friendships are bad, but because everything flows from it. What you let in has a way of flowing back out—through your words, your decisions, and your identity.

Guarding your heart doesn't mean being cold or closed off. It means being *intentional.* Asking:

- o   Is this relationship helping me grow closer to God?

- o   Is this friendship healthy and respectful?

- o   Is this media, music, or habit shaping me to be more like Jesus— or less?

And sometimes, guarding your heart means *letting go* of things that feel good in the moment but pull you away from your purpose. That's not weakness—
it's wisdom.

 # Key Scriptures

Proverbs 4:23 (NIV)

"Above all else, guard your heart, for everything you do flows from it."

   What goes into your heart determines what comes out in your life.

Jeremiah 17:9 (NLT)

"The human heart is the most deceitful of all things, and desperately wicked. Who really knows how bad it is?"

   Your heart needs guidance—not blind trust.

Ezekiel 36:26 (NIV)

"I will give you a new heart and put a new spirit in you; I will remove from you your heart of stone and give you a heart of flesh."

   God doesn't want a hardened heart—He wants a *healed, alive, sensitive one.*

Living It Out

- o **Check what's shaping your heart.**
  Is what you're watching, listening to, or following leading you toward peace or confusion? Toward hope or comparison? Be honest.

- o **Ask better questions.**
  Instead of *"How far is too far?"* or *"Is this bad?"* try asking: *"Will this bring me closer to Jesus—or pull me away?"*

- o **Don't confuse "guarding" with "blocking."**
  It's okay to love deeply. But guard your heart with prayer and wisdom, not fear. Set boundaries, not walls.

- o **Let God lead your feelings.**
  Your emotions aren't bad, but they need a compass. Invite God to guide your desires so you're not just following your heart—you're following *Him.*

- o **Stay soft. Stay strong.**
  Being guarded doesn't mean being bitter. Ask God to help you protect your heart *without losing your tenderness.*

Journal Prompt

- o Are there relationships or habits in my life that I need to re-evaluate?

- o When have I hardened my heart instead of guarding it?

- o What would it look like to guard my heart with God's help, not just my own strength?

- o What's one area of my life I can surrender to Jesus today?

This Week's Challenge

This week, do a "heart check."
Take 15–20 minutes and write down the things that are taking up space in your heart—friendships, feelings, habits, media, even secret struggles. Then ask: *Are these drawing me closer to God… or pulling me away?*

If something isn't helping you grow, it's okay to create space. Let God be the guardian of your heart—He'll protect it better than anyone else can.

Let's Pray

Dear God,

Sometimes I don't know what to do with my heart. It feels too big, too fragile, too messy. I want to love well, but I also want to be wise. I've been hurt, disappointed, and even tempted to shut down altogether.

Teach me how to guard my heart without hardening it. Help me stay soft but strong, open but discerning. Show me what to let in, what to release, and how to trust You with the deepest parts of who I am.

Lead my heart, Lord—don't let me follow it blindly. I want to follow You instead.

In Jesus name,
Amen.

Chapter 36:

Speak Life –Communicate with Confidence

Ever had a moment where you *wanted* to speak up but didn't? Maybe your heart was pounding, your hands were sweating, and your brain said, "Say something!" but your mouth said, "Nope."

Yep, been there.

Or maybe you've had *this* moment: You finally said something, but it came out *totally wrong.* Like, it was supposed to be honest and kind... but somehow it came out snappy and awkward. And then you're lying in bed at 11:37 p.m.
replaying the whole convo in your head like a movie you wish you could rewrite.

Let's talk about that. Let's talk about learning to speak with *confidence, grace, and truth*—because your voice matters. And God actually has a lot to say about *how* we speak.

Story Time: The Great Friend-Group Text Disaster

So one time, I was in a group text with two of my besties, and things were getting spicy. One of them—let's call her Ava—was clearly upset about something the other one—let's say Jess—had said earlier that day.

Instead of talking to Jess directly, Ava sent a super vague message to the group like, "Some people just don't know when to keep their opinions to themselves" Jess responded with "Umm... what's that supposed to mean?" and I... froze. I didn't want to take sides. So I said nothing.

Spoiler alert: That made it worse.

146

Later, Ava texted me privately and was like, "Thanks for backing me up." And Jess? She ghosted me for three days.

Moral of the story: *Miscommunication = mess*. Silence in the wrong moment can hurt just as much as saying the wrong thing. That day, I learned the hard way that communication takes courage—and clarity.

Truth Talk: Why God Cares About Our Words

Words are powerful. Like really powerful. They can start wars, heal hearts, or make someone's whole day with just a single sentence.

– Colossians 4:6 (NIV): *"Let your conversation be always full of grace, seasoned with salt, so that you may know how to answer everyone."*

Let's break that down.

- o **"Full of grace"** means our words should be kind, patient, and forgiving—not snarky, gossipy, or rude.

- o **"Seasoned with salt"** means they should also be flavorful and wise—truthful, not bland or fake.

- o And **"know how to answer"** reminds us to think before we speak. Because not every situation needs a mic drop moment... sometimes it just needs love.

Your words matter to God—because they have the power to bring life or damage. The choice is ours.

Why We Stay Silent (and Why We Shouldn't)

So why is it so hard to speak up sometimes?

- o We're afraid people won't like us.

- o We don't want to start drama.

- o We doubt if what we have to say is even *worth saying.*

But girl, your voice is valuable. Not just when you say something funny or helpful—but when you speak truth, stand up for someone, or share what's really on your heart.

God doesn't want us to be loud and bossy—but He does want us to be bold and loving.

The Secret Power of Listening

Here's a little communication secret: *Great communicators aren't just good talkers—they're amazing listeners.*

When you actually listen—like really, listen—you're telling someone: "You matter. I care. I'm not just waiting to talk."

Jesus was the best listener. He asked questions. He heard people's hearts. He noticed what others ignored.

So before you speak, ask: "Have I listened long enough to truly understand?"

Journal Prompt

Grab a notebook or the notes app on your phone and reflect:

- o   Think about the last time you didn't say what you really meant. What do you wish you had said?

- o   Is there someone you need to speak up to—with truth and grace?

- o   Are there times when you talk more than you listen?

Write out a prayer or a practice convo if you need to. Seriously, it helps!

This Week's Challenge

Choose one person to encourage this week with your words. Say something that builds them up—whether it's face-to-face, over text, or in a handwritten note (yes, those still exist!).

Also: Practice *active listening.*
Put down your phone, make eye contact, and *listen without interrupting.*
You'll be amazed at how different people respond when they feel heard.

Bonus points if you *both* speak life and listen well in the same conversation.

 Let's Pray

Dear God,

Thank You for giving me a voice. Sometimes I feel scared to use it, or I mess up and say the wrong thing. Help me to speak with confidence, truth, and kindness. Fill my words with grace and my heart with courage. Teach me to be a better listener, and show me how to build others up with what I say. Let everything I speak reflect Your love.

In Jesus name,
Amen.

You don't have to be the loudest girl in the room to make an impact.
You just have to speak with love.
You don't have to be perfect with your words.
You just have to be *willing to grow.*

And girl—you're growing beautifully.

## Chapter 37

Speak Truth (Even If Your Voice Shakes)

Speak the truth in love, even when it's hard
(Ephesians 4:15)

Your heart's pounding.
Your palms are sweaty.
And every fiber in you is screaming, *"Stay quiet. Don't rock the boat."*

But deep down... you know you need to say something.
Maybe it's calling out a lie.
Maybe it's defending someone.
Maybe it's finally speaking up for yourself.

But it's scary, right?

We live in a world where speaking truth can feel risky. People might misunderstand. Get offended. Push back. Or worse—stop talking to you altogether.

But here's what's even riskier: staying silent when God is nudging you to speak.

God's Truth

Ephesians 4:15 says:

"Instead, speaking the truth in love, we will grow to become in every respect the mature body of Him who is the head, that is, Christ."

Did you catch that? Truth + Love = Growth.
It's not just about what you say—it's *how* you say it.

Speaking truth is more than just boldness. It's about *courage with compassion.*

It's telling your friend that gossip is hurtful… but with kindness. It's standing up against what's wrong… without becoming harsh or bitter. It's choosing honesty in a world that loves comfort and filters and half-truths.

Jesus never watered down truth—but He never used it as a weapon either. He spoke directly, clearly, and always with love. And if He could do that while facing betrayal, misunderstanding, and even death—you can do it too, even with shaky hands and a trembling voice.

Key Scriptures:

Ephesians 4:15 (NIV)

"Instead, speaking the truth in love, we will grow to become in every respect the mature body of Him who is the head, that is, Christ."
Truth without love can hurt. Love without truth can mislead. We need both.

Proverbs 31:8 (NLT)

"Speak up for those who cannot speak for themselves; ensure justice for those being crushed."
Sometimes your voice is the one that sets others free.

2 Timothy 1:7 (ESV)

"For God gave us a spirit not of fear but of power and love and self-control."
You don't have to feel brave to be bold in truth.

Living It Out

- **Check your heart before you speak.**
  Are you speaking to help—or to prove a point? Truth should never be about pride or power. Ask God to purify your motive first.

- **Don't confuse silence with peace.**
  Avoiding hard conversations might keep things "quiet," but real peace comes from truth. Speak gently—but don't avoid what needs to be said.

o   **Practice first—pray first.**
    Before having a difficult convo, write it out. Talk to God about it.
    Ask Him to help you speak with grace and clarity.

o   **Be okay with not being liked by everyone.**
    Even when you speak with love, some people won't like what you
    say. That doesn't mean you were wrong. It means you were obedient.

o   **Remember: Your voice matters.**
    You don't need a microphone or a crowd. You just need one
    moment of courage. And God will meet you right there.

 Journal Prompt

o   When have I stayed quiet because I was afraid to speak truth?

o   Is there something I need to say to someone in love?

o   What would it look like to speak up with both courage and kindness?

o   Have I ever used truth without love—or love without truth?

This Week's Challenge

This week, ask God to show you one moment where you can speak truth in love.
It might be a conversation with a friend, a moment to stand up for what's
right, or even a loving correction. When the opportunity comes, don't run
from it. Speak—*even if your voice shakes.*

Let's Pray

Dear God,

*You know how hard it is for me to speak up sometimes. I want to be kind. I
don't want to upset anyone. But I also don't want to stay silent when You're calling
me to speak. Give me courage to say what needs to be said—and compassion
to say it in the right way. Help me speak truth with love, not fear. And when
my voice shakes, remind me that You are strong even when I feel small. Use
my words to bring healing, not hurt. Truth, not tension. Grace, not guilt.*

In Jesus' name,
Amen.

## Chapter 38

Anchor Yourself in the Word

Let's be real—life can feel like a whirlwind. School drama, friend drama, family drama… *internal* drama. Some days you're riding high and feeling like you've got it all together, and other days you're crying over a broken nail and an unanswered text message (we've all been there). So how do we stay steady when everything around and inside us is constantly shifting?

Simple. We anchor ourselves in the Word.

Life Feels Wavy—God's Word is Steady

Picture this: You're on a tiny boat in the middle of the ocean. Waves are crashing, the wind is wild, and you're gripping the sides for dear life. Suddenly, someone hands you a strong, steady anchor. You drop it, and—whoosh— the boat settles. It's still floating, but it's no longer being tossed around.

That's what the Bible does for your heart.

Psalm 119:105 says, *"Your word is a lamp for my feet, a light on my path."* When you feel unsure, God's Word helps you see where to go next. It's not a giant spotlight revealing your whole future, but it is a lamp—just enough light for the next step. And that's all you really need.

Start or End Your Day with the Word

Now before you panic, this isn't about reading five chapters of Leviticus every morning before sunrise. Nope. Anchoring yourself in the Word can be as simple as reading one verse and letting it sink into your heart.

Pro tip: Pick a verse, write it on a sticky note, and stick it somewhere you'll see it—like your bathroom mirror or your phone lock screen.

Want to know the secret sauce? Don't just read it—live it. Let it shape your thoughts, your words, your actions. Ask: "How can I walk this out today?"

Here's an example:
Read: "Be kind to one another, tenderhearted, forgiving one another, as God in Christ forgave you." **(Ephesians 4:32)**
Live it: Offer grace to the classmate who totally ignored you at lunch. Again.

Personal Story Time

There was a time in 9th grade when I felt completely invisible. Like I could disappear from my friend group and no one would notice. I remember grabbing my Bible in frustration and randomly flipping to Psalm 139. And wow—it hit me: *"You are fearfully and wonderfully made."* That one line stuck with me.

So I wrote it on a note and taped it inside my locker. Every time I opened it to grab my books or a snack (okay, mostly snacks), I saw it. And little by little, God reminded me of who I am. Not forgotten. Not invisible. *Known and loved.*

Journal Prompt

o   What's one verse that has encouraged you before?

o   How could starting your day with God's Word change your mindset?

o   Where can you put Scripture reminders in your daily routine (mirror, locker, phone, planner)?

This Week's Challenge

Pick ONE verse this week that speaks to you. Write it down. Put it somewhere visible. And then? Do your best to live it out for the next 7 days. Watch how even one verse can make a big difference.

 Let's Pray

Dear Heavenly Father,

Thank You for giving me Your Word. It's steady, trustworthy, and full of truth. Help me to crave it more than distractions, to read it with an open heart, and to live it boldly. When life feels chaotic, remind me to anchor my soul in what never changes—You.

In Jesus name
Amen

## Chapter 39

Stay Connected to the Source

Have you ever had your phone die right when you needed it most? Maybe you were about to post the perfect selfie, or you were in the middle of texting your bestie about a major life crisis (you know, like running out of lip gloss). Then—black screen. No warning. No goodbye. Just... dead.

Why? Because you weren't connected to the charger.

Just like your phone needs a steady power source to stay alive and useful, *your heart needs connection to Jesus to thrive.* He is your power source. Your lifeline. Your peace in chaos and your joy in the mundane.

"I Am the Vine..."

In **John 15:5**, Jesus says, *"I am the vine; you are the branches. If you remain in me and I in you, you will bear much fruit; apart from me you can do nothing."*

That's a beautiful picture. A branch doesn't try really hard to grow grapes. It doesn't hustle or stress. It just *stays connected* to the vine, and the vine takes care of the rest.

Your job? Stay close to Jesus. Let Him fuel you, guide you, and strengthen you.

How Do I Stay Connected?

This isn't about being in church 24/7 or having a perfect quiet time every morning (although those things are awesome!). It's about being aware of God's presence—*all day long*. It's about inviting Him into the little moments, not just the big ones.

Here's how to do it:

- o Whisper a prayer before your math test.

- o Thank Him when your favorite song comes on.

- o Ask for patience when your sibling pushes every single button you have.

- o Say "Help me, Jesus" when you feel overwhelmed.

The best part? He hears *every single one* of your whispers.

Tiny Prayers, Big Connection

Let's get something straight: You don't need fancy words to talk to God. You don't have to sound like a Bible scholar or a pastor. Jesus isn't grading your grammar—He just wants your heart.

You can talk to Him like you would your closest friend:

- o "God, I'm nervous."

- o "Jesus, thank You for that hug."

- o "Lord, help me not lose my cool right now."

Think of it like an ongoing conversation—little check-ins with the One who never stops listening.

Personal Story Time

There was a season when I felt super disconnected from God. I thought maybe I had to *do more*—read more, pray longer, be better. But then I remembered a verse: *"Draw near to God and He will draw near to you."* **(James 4:8)**

So I started whispering quick prayers while brushing my teeth, walking to class, or scrolling social media. It wasn't about performance—it was about *presence.* And slowly, I felt my heart shift. I didn't feel so alone anymore. I felt seen. Heard. Held.

 ## Journal Prompts

o What does "staying connected to Jesus" look like for you right now?

o What's one small way you can check in with God throughout your day?

o What lies have you believed about prayer that you need to let go of?

 ## This Week's Challenge

For the next 3 days, try whispering one-sentence prayers to Jesus—morning, noon, and night. They don't have to be perfect. They just have to be *real.* Keep track of what you notice. Hint: You might just feel closer to Him than ever before.

Let's Pray

Dear Heavenly Father,

I want to stay connected to You. You are my strength, my peace, my hope. Teach me to talk to You throughout the day—to lean on You, listen to You, and live in step with You. Even when I feel weak or distracted, remind me You're just one whisper away.

In Jesus name,
Amen

Chapter 40:
Choose Community Over Cliques

You've seen it—and maybe even felt it. The lunch tables divided like invisible lines in a battlefield. The "cool girls" on one end, talking in hushed tones and tossing perfect hair. The athletes over there. The artsy ones huddled in their corner. And you? Maybe you've asked yourself, *Where do I fit in?*

Spoiler alert: You were never meant to *fit in*—you were meant to *belong*. And there's a big difference.

What Culture Says vs. What God Says

Culture says:
"Find your people. Stick with your clique. Keep others out."

God says **(Romans 12:5)**:
"So in Christ we, though many, form one body, and each member belongs to all the others."

Read that again: *You belong*. Not because you look the same, talk the same, or have the same taste in music—but because Jesus made you part of *His family*. And His family doesn't run on popularity points or social rankings.

God's Family > Exclusive Friend Groups

Let's be real: Cliques are built on fear. The fear of not being enough. The fear of being left out. The fear of standing alone. So we cling to people who look like us, think like us, act like us—hoping it'll make us feel secure.

But guess what? Security doesn't come from a clique. It comes from community. The kind where you're *seen and loved*, not just tolerated.

God's kind of friendship is:

- o   Rooted in love, not status.

- o   Built on truth, not gossip.

- o   Fueled by encouragement, not comparison.

Find Friends Who Help You Grow

The Bible says in **Proverbs 13:2**0, *"Walk with the wise and become wise."* Translation: Your friends matter. Big time.

Ask yourself:

- o   Do my friends help me love Jesus more?

- o   Are they kind, honest, and strong?

- o   Do they celebrate who I am without asking me to shrink?

If not, it might be time to gently step away from the clique and seek out community instead.

You weren't made to do life alone. And you definitely weren't made to compete for a spot at someone else's table. Jesus already gave you a seat at His.

Journal Prompts

- o   Have I ever felt left out or judged by a friend group? How did that impact me?

- o   What qualities do I want in godly friends?

- o   How can I be a community-builder instead of a clique-follower?

This Week's Challenge

This week, look for someone who's sitting alone—or just seems left out. Invite them to join you. Sit with them. Smile at them. Be the kind of friend you wish you had on your hardest day. You might be the answer to someone else's silent prayer.

Let's Pray

Dear Heavenly Father,

Thank You for making me part of Your family. Help me let go of my need to "fit in" and instead build real community with people who love You. Show me friends who help me grow, and help me be that kind of friend too. Give me the courage to include others the way You include me.

In Jesus name,
Amen

Chapter 41:
Fail Forward with Grace

Let's talk about something nobody loves, but everybody deals with: messing up. Whether it's snapping at your sibling, blowing a test you actually studied for, or saying something you instantly wish you could take back—failure happens.

And it stings. Hard.

But here's the truth the world won't tell you: *Failure doesn't disqualify you. Grace does the opposite—it picks you up and propels you forward.*

💬 What Culture Says vs. What God Says

Culture says:
"Don't mess up. Be flawless. One failure, and you're done."

God says **(2 Corinthians 12:9)**:
"My grace is sufficient for you, for my power is made perfect in weakness."

That means even when you totally blow it, God isn't shaking His head in disappointment. He's reaching out with love, saying, *"I've got you. Let's try again."*

Mess-Ups Are a Part of Growing Up

Failing doesn't make you a failure. It makes you human.

We all have off days, emotional outbursts, wrong choices, or seasons where we drift. But here's what makes the difference: What you do next.

Do you:

- o   Hide it?

- o   Beat yourself up?

- o   Pretend like nothing happened?

Or do you run to Jesus, hand Him your mess, and let Him turn it into something beautiful?

Failing forward means *you keep going*. You fall toward God, not away from Him.

Grace Isn't a Free Pass—It's a Fresh Start

Grace doesn't say, "Do whatever you want."

It says, "Even when you fall short, you're still loved, still chosen, and still called."

Peter denied Jesus three times, and Jesus still built the church on him. David made some major mistakes, and God still called him "a man after My own heart."

Your failures don't surprise God. But your willingness to come back to Him? That's powerful.

Flip the Script

Instead of:

- o   "I'm such a mess-up," say: *"God's not done with me yet."*

- o   "I'll never get it right," say: *"His grace covers this too."*

- o   "I failed," say: *"I'm learning, growing, and getting stronger."*

The enemy wants you stuck in shame. But God wants you walking in freedom.

# Journal Prompts

What's one recent failure that's been weighing on your heart?

How did you respond in that moment?

What does God say about you in *that exact place?*

# This Week's Challenge

Write 2 **Corinthians 12:9** somewhere you'll see it—your mirror, planner, or phone background. When you mess up (and you will!), read it out loud. Then take a deep breath, talk to Jesus, and get back up. Grace is already waiting.

Let's Pray

Dear Heavenly Father,

thank You that I don't have to be perfect to be loved by You. Help me to stop hiding my failures and start bringing them to You. When I fall, remind me that Your grace lifts me up. I want to grow forward, even in the messy moments.

In Jesus name,
Amen

## Chapter 42

Live on Purpose, Not for Popularity

Let's be real: popularity can feel like everything. Who likes your posts. Who notices your outfit. Who includes you in the group chat.

But here's the catch—it's a game that never ends. The moment you chase popularity, you're stuck trying to keep everyone happy... and spoiler alert: that's exhausting.

But you? You weren't created to live for likes.
You were created *on purpose, for a purpose*.

What Culture Says vs. What God Says

Culture says:
"Fit in. Be liked. Do what it takes to stay relevant."

God says **(Ephesians 2:10)**:
"For we are God's masterpiece, created in Christ Jesus to do good works, which God prepared in advance for us to do."

God's not asking you to be the most popular girl in school.
He's asking you to be the *light*—right where you are. To use your gifts, your story, and your heart to make a difference.

What If "Small" Is Actually Huge?

Sometimes we think purpose has to look flashy—like being the next viral influencer, headlining a youth event, or starting a global nonprofit at 15.

But guess what? Purpose is often quiet.

It's:

o   Smiling at the new girl who looks nervous at lunch.

o   Sending a "thinking of you" text to a friend who's struggling.

o   Helping your younger sibling with homework (even if they're super annoying).

Every kind thing done in love counts. Big time.

Chasing Popularity Is a Trap

Here's what happens when we start living *for* popularity:

o   We shrink to fit in.

o   We pretend to be someone we're not.

o   We end up drained, confused, and honestly… kind of lonely.

But when we live *on* purpose:

o   We stand tall in who we are.

o   We use our gifts boldly, even if others don't "get it."

o   We find joy in making a difference, not just making noise.

You Have Something the World Needs

Yes, you.

Whether you're artsy, sporty, super organized, a quiet thinker, or the class clown—*God put something inside you that's meant to bless others.*

So instead of asking:

"Will people like me?"

Start asking:

"How can I serve today?"

"What can I give instead of just get?"
"Who needs encouragement that I can offer?"

That's how you live *on purpose*. And honestly? That's way more fulfilling than any number of likes.

 ## Journal Prompts

- o What's one gift or talent you know God has given you?

- o How are you using it—or how *could* you use it—to bless someone this week?

- o Where have you been tempted to live for popularity? What would living on purpose look like in that area?

This Week's Challenge

Write Ephesians 2:10 on a sticky note or your phone's lock screen. Then choose *one way today* to use a gift you've been given—your creativity, your encouragement, your listening ear—to love someone well.

It doesn't have to be big. It just has to be *real.*

Let's Pray

Dear Heavenly Father,

Help me not to chase popularity, but to chase You. I want to live on purpose, not for the approval of others. Show me how to use the gifts You've placed in me—no matter how small they seem—to shine Your light in this world.

In Jesus name,
Amen

Chapter 43:
Stand Firm When the World Shakes

Ever felt like everything around you is shifting—friendships, social media trends, expectations, your own emotions? One minute you're feeling confident, and the next, you're second-guessing every little thing.

Yeah. Life can feel shaky.

But here's the good news: you don't have to shake with it.

You can stand steady, even when the world feels like it's spinning.
How? By staying rooted in something (and Someone) that never changes.

The World Shifts—God Doesn't

One day it's cool to be kind, the next day sarcasm is trending. One month you're "in," the next you're ignored.
Trends change. People change. Feelings change.

But God's truth?
Solid. Secure. Always steady.

"Be strong and courageous. Do not be afraid; do not be discouraged, for the Lord your God will be with you wherever you go."
— **Joshua 1:9**

Whether you're walking into a new school, facing peer pressure, or wrestling with who you are—you're not alone. And you're not meant to follow the crowd just to feel safe. You're meant to *stand firm*, even when standing firm makes you stand out.

Know Your Non-Negotiables

Let's talk boundaries.

Not the boring, rule-based kind, but the "I know who I am and what I believe" kind.

Here's what that might look like:

- o   "I won't gossip, even if everyone around me is."

- o   "I choose modesty, even when fashion says 'less is more.'"

- o   "I won't compromise my worth to get someone's attention."

- o   "I believe in Jesus, even when that makes me different."

You don't have to announce your non-negotiables on a t-shirt.
But you *do* need to know them—and *hold them tight*.

Write them down. Memorize them. Let them guide your choices when the pressure is on.

Standing Firm Isn't Always Easy

Sometimes standing firm means:

- o   Saying no when it would be easier to say yes.

- o   Being left out because you didn't go along with the crowd.

- o   Being misunderstood for choosing faith over fitting in.

But hear this: You are not missing out when you stand for truth.
You are *setting yourself apart*. You are building a life on solid ground instead of sinking sand.

What Helps You Stay Grounded?

Here are a few things that can keep your footing firm when life shakes:

- o   **Scripture:** Read it, memorize it, live it.

o   **Let's Pray:** Whisper your fears and ask for courage.

o   **Wise friends:** Surround yourself with people who remind you of truth.

o   **Worship:** Turn your eyes off the storm and back on your Savior.

 Journal Prompts

o   What are 3 non-negotiables in your life right now?

o   When was a time you stood firm even when it was hard?

o   Where do you feel tempted to compromise—and how can you choose truth instead?

This Week's Challenge

Write Joshua 1:9 on a sticky note and put it somewhere visible—your locker, mirror, or phone wallpaper. Let it remind you that you're not alone and you're stronger than you feel.

Then take 10 minutes to write down your top 3 non-negotiables—those unshakable truths or values that you want to live by no matter what. Revisit them when life tries to shake you.

Let's Pray

Dear Heavenly Father,

Help me to stand strong, even when it feels like everything around me is changing. Root me in Your Word. Remind me that You're always with me. Show me how to live boldly, with courage and truth, even when it's not popular. I want to be unshakable in You.

In Jesus name,
Amen

## PART 5

STEPPING
Into Your Strength

Buildig Resilience,
Courge and Purpose

## Chapter 44

Shine Bright — Living Your Faith Out Loud

"You are the light of the world. A town built on a hill cannot be hidden… let your light shine before others, that they may see your good deeds and glorify your Father in heaven."
— Matthew 5:14–16 (NIV)

Quiet confidence and walking with God in your own way

"The Lord will fight for you; you need only to be still."
— Exodus 14:14 (NIV)

What If I'm Not Loud or Outgoing?

Here's something I wish more people said out loud:
You don't have to be the loudest voice in the room to have the strongest faith.

Some people shout their beliefs from rooftops (literally or online). Others quietly show up, live with kindness, and love deeply in the background. One isn't more "spiritual" than the other. They're just *different expressions* of boldness.

This chapter is for the ones who might feel like their quieter faith somehow doesn't count. Newsflash: *it does.* Big time.

What Is Boldness, Really?

When we hear the word *bold*, we usually picture someone fearless, outspoken, maybe even a little dramatic. But godly boldness isn't about volume or personality. It's about *knowing who you belong to and living like it*—with quiet confidence, even when no one else is watching.

Jesus was bold when He stood up for the woman caught in adultery. Esther was bold when she risked everything to save her people. Mary was bold when she said "yes" to God even though it cost her everything.

None of them were chasing attention. They were just obedient. That's the real kind of bold that lasts.

Walking with God in Your Own Way

Maybe you're more introverted. Maybe big crowds freak you out. Maybe you'd rather write someone a heartfelt note than speak on stage. Good news: God made you that way *on purpose*.

God doesn't need you to change your personality—He just wants your heart.

Walking with God in your own way might look like:

- o   Quiet moments in your journal, praying and processing your faith

- o   Sending an encouraging text that lifts someone's whole day

- o   Saying a small prayer before every class or big decision

- o   Choosing kindness in the middle of drama

- o   Serving behind the scenes without needing the spotlight

Don't underestimate the impact of your *everyday obedience*. God does powerful things through quiet faithfulness.

You Can Be Both Soft and Strong

Let's throw out the idea that boldness = being brash, loud, or aggressive. Jesus Himself was gentle and lowly, yet He flipped tables and conquered sin and death.

Boldness isn't about being loud. It's about being rooted.
Rooted in love. Rooted in truth. Rooted in who God says you are.

Quiet confidence is choosing not to shrink back or show off. It's standing your ground with grace, knowing who's got your back (hint: it's the Creator of the universe).

"Let your gentleness be evident to all. The Lord is near."
— **Philippians 4:5 (NIV)**

You Are a Light, Even in the Background

Sometimes the loudest faith isn't the most effective.
Sometimes it's the consistent, quiet witness that softens hearts.

Think about a candle in a dark room. It doesn't need to scream to be seen. It just shines.

You shine when you:

- o   Refuse to gossip even when others do

- o   Forgive someone who hurt you deeply

- o   Share a piece of your story with someone who's struggling

- o   Stay close to Jesus even when no one else seems to care

Your quiet strength is a light. Don't hide it or think it's not enough. The world desperately needs it.

"You are the light of the world... let your light shine before others, that they may see your good deeds and glorify your Father in heaven."
— **Matthew 5:14, 16 (NIV)**

How to Share Your Beliefs with Love, Not Fear

There's a difference between *sharing your faith and shoving your faith.*
Jesus never guilt-tripped people into following Him—He invited them with love, grace, and truth. That's your blueprint.

Here's how to do it well:

o   **Be Relatable, Not Perfect**
People connect with real, not flawless. Share your struggles, not just your wins. It shows that faith is for everyone—not just the "put-together."

o   **Ask Questions, Don't Just Preach**
If someone is curious about your faith, ask about their beliefs too. Listen without judgment. Love always listens.

o   **Let Your Life Be the Mic**
The way you treat people, speak to others, and live day-to-day will say more about your faith than a 10-minute speech ever could.

o   **Speak Up When Prompted**
If the Holy Spirit nudges you to encourage someone, pray for them, or share a truth—do it. You don't have to have perfect words. Just be obedient.

Scripture Power: Matthew 5:14–16 Explained

Let's slow this down:

"You are the light of the world."
Jesus didn't say *you might be* a light. He said you are. That means you already have what it takes. You carry His light inside you—and the world needs it.

"A town built on a hill cannot be hidden."
When you live like Jesus, it's noticeable. You're set apart. And while that might feel awkward sometimes, it's actually beautiful. You were never meant to blend in.

"Let your light shine before others…"
It's not about being flashy—it's about being faithful. Shine with purpose, not performance.

"…that they may see your good deeds and glorify your Father in heaven."
The goal? To point people to Jesus, not to you. Your light is a reflection of Him. So when you're kind, loving, bold, or joyful—that's Jesus shining through you.

 ## Journal Prompts

- o   What's one area of your life where you've been hiding your light?

- o   Who in your world might need to see the light of Jesus through you?

- o   What's holding you back from being bold in your faith?

- o   How can you reflect Jesus in small, everyday ways—online and offline?

This Week's Challenge

This week, be intentional about one way you can shine *your light*. Whether it's sharing encouragement with a friend, praying before lunch in public, or posting something faith-inspired on social—take the leap. Even the smallest spark can light up someone else's darkness.

 ## Let's Pray

Dear Heavenly Father,

Thank You for being the Light in my life. Help me to shine brightly for You— even when it's uncomfortable. Give me boldness without fear, and help me share Your love with grace and truth. May my life reflect who You are in all I do.

In Jesus name,
Amen

## Chapter 45

Purpose Over Pressure

"For we are God's masterpiece. He has created us anew in Christ Jesus, so we can do the good things He planned for us long ago."
— **Ephesians 2:10 (NLT)**

The Pressure Is Real

Let's just say it out loud: being a teen girl today can feel like living under a constant spotlight.
Get straight A's.
Make varsity.
Be the nicest, prettiest, funniest girl in the room.
Crush it on social media.
Make your family proud.
Never mess up.

Whew. No wonder so many girls feel like they're not enough.

But guess what? God never asked you to be perfect. He didn't create you to perform—He created you on purpose and for a purpose.

Let's talk about what it means to stop chasing perfection... and start living out your calling.

Letting Go of Perfectionism and Performance

Perfectionism is sneaky. It can sound like:

o   "If I don't do this flawlessly, I've failed."

o   "I have to make everyone happy."

o   "I'm only as valuable as my achievements."

But here's the truth: God isn't impressed by your perfection—He's drawn to your *authenticity*. He's not keeping a scoreboard. He's after your heart.

When you live to impress others, you end up exhausted and empty. When you live to honor God, you find freedom.

"Am I now trying to win the approval of human beings, or of God? Or am I trying to please people? If I were still trying to please people, I would not be a servant of Christ."
— **Galatians 1:10 (NIV)**

You don't have to strive to be someone you're not. You don't have to carry the weight of being "perfect." Jesus already lived perfectly on your behalf. Your job now? Walk in the freedom He died to give you.

Discovering Your Calling and Gifts

Here's a little secret: Your purpose isn't some mystical, out-of-reach thing that you'll only "figure out" when you're 30.

Your purpose starts now—right where you are.

God has given you *gifts, talents,* and *personality* traits that are no accident. Whether you're artistic, athletic, organized, funny, deep-thinking, musical, nurturing, or techy—God wired you with intentional design.

Your calling is where your *God-given gifts* meet the *world's needs.*

So if you're wondering how to discover your purpose, try asking:

o   What am I passionate about?

o   What am I naturally good at?

o   What breaks my heart or fires me up?

o   What do other people say I'm good at?

And most importantly: "How can I use these things to serve others and glorify God?"

"Each of you should use whatever gift you have received to serve others, as faithful stewards of God's grace…"
— 1 Peter 4:10 (NIV)

You don't need a platform or a title to live out your calling. You just need a heart willing to say, "God, use me."

Serving God Right Where You Are

You don't have to wait until you're older, smarter, or "more spiritual" to be used by God. He uses teens all the time—just look at David, Esther, Mary, and Timothy.

God loves to work through people who say yes, even when they feel small.

Here's what serving God right now could look like:

- Encouraging a friend who's going through a hard time

- Volunteering at your church or school

- Starting a Bible study at lunch or in a group chat

- Using your creativity (art, music, writing, etc.) to inspire others

- Being the kind of friend who listens, prays, and shows up

Your everyday life is full of opportunities to shine His light and reflect His love. You don't have to change the whole world—just be faithful in your corner of it.

 Key Scriptures

Ephesians 2:10 (NLT)
"For we are God's masterpiece. He has created us anew in Christ Jesus, so we can do the good things He planned for us long ago."
You are a masterpiece, not a mistake. God handcrafted you for good things. He's already got a plan—your job is to walk in it.

Romans 12:6 (NLT)

"In His grace, God has given us different gifts for doing certain things well."

Your gift might not look like hers—and that's the point! Your unique mix of talents is by design.

Colossians 3:23 (NIV)

"Whatever you do, work at it with all your heart, as working for the Lord, not for human masters."

Whether you're leading worship or doing algebra homework, do it for God. He sees it all, and it all matters.

Journal Prompts

o   Where do I feel pressure to be perfect? How can I invite God into that area?

o   What gifts or passions has God given me?

o   How could I use those gifts to serve others?

o   What does it look like to choose purpose over pressure in my everyday life?

This Week's Challenge

This week, take one step toward purpose:

o   Say no to one thing that's rooted in people-pleasing

o   Try something new that aligns with your passions

o   Ask God to show you a small way to serve someone near you

Remember: Faithfulness in the small things prepares you for the big things.

Let's Pray

Dear Heavenly Father,

Thank You for creating me with intention and purpose. Help me let go of the pressure to perform and live to please You, not people. Show me the gifts You've placed inside me, and teach me how to use them to make a difference right where I am. I want to live on purpose—for You.

In Jesus name, Amen

## Chapter 46

Prayer That Changes Everything

"The prayer of a righteous person is powerful and effective."
— James 5:16b (NIV)

"But I Don't Know How to Pray..."

Let's be real: prayer can feel awkward sometimes.

You sit down, close your eyes, fold your hands... and then what?
Your mind wanders. You suddenly remember that math test you forgot to study for. You wonder if you're saying the "right" words. You feel silly or distracted or... nothing at all.

Sound familiar?

The truth is, prayer isn't about being perfect—it's about being *present*. It's not a religious performance; it's a real relationship. And God? He's not grading you on your grammar or how many "Dear Lord"s you can squeeze into 30 seconds. He just wants your heart.

Let's explore how prayer can go from feeling stiff and confusing... to becoming the most powerful, personal part of your faith.

How to Pray When You Feel Stuck or Unsure

Here's a big truth: *You don't have to have it all together to talk to God.*

In fact, some of the best prayers in the Bible were just honest cries for help.

- o   "Lord, help me!"

- o   "I believe—help my unbelief."

o   "Teach me Your ways."

You don't need fancy words. You don't have to speak in "King James" English. Just be you.

Here are some ways to pray when you're not sure what to say:

o   **Be honest.**
    Tell God exactly how you feel—even if you're confused, mad, tired, or doubting. He can handle it.

o   **Start simple.**
    Try one-sentence prayers like:

    "Jesus, I need You right now."
    "God, give me peace today."
    "Help me be kind, even when I don't feel like it."

o   **Use Scripture.**
    Read a verse and turn it into a prayer. For example, if you read "The Lord is my shepherd…" **(Psalm 23)**, you might pray, "God, lead me today. Help me trust You."

o   **Write it out.**
    Prayer journaling is a great way to untangle your thoughts and connect with God on paper. No filter needed—just pour out your heart.

Listening to God's Voice in Your Life

Prayer isn't just about talking—it's also about *listening*.

But what does that actually look like?

God speaks in all kinds of ways:

o   Through His Word (the Bible)

o   Through the Holy Spirit's gentle nudges

o   Through wise mentors, friends, or teachers

o   Through moments of peace or conviction in your heart

Listening to God takes practice, just like learning a friend's voice over time. The more time you spend with Him, the more clearly you'll recognize when He's speaking.

And spoiler alert: if you're waiting for a loud, booming voice from the sky, don't be discouraged. God often speaks in whispers—in stillness, quiet moments, and through His Word.

"My sheep listen to my voice; I know them, and they follow me."
— **John 10:27 (NIV)**

Start by asking Him, "God, what are You trying to show me today?" Then be still. Watch for peace. Pay attention to what Scripture says. And trust that He's guiding you—even when it feels subtle.

Creating a Daily Prayer Habit That Feels Real and Personal

Let's face it—life is busy. Between school, sports, friends, scrolling, and surviving each day, it can feel impossible to carve out time to pray.

But here's the good news: prayer isn't about a time slot. It's about connection.

That said, building a habit of prayer helps anchor your faith. It becomes less about squeezing God in and more about keeping Him at the center.

Here are some practical ways to make prayer part of your daily life:

- **Morning Moments**
  Start your day with a 1-minute prayer while brushing your teeth, walking to school, or sipping your coffee. Something like: "God, help me walk with You today. Open my eyes to what You're doing."

- **Prayer Prompts**
  Attach prayer to something you already do. Every time you open your locker? Say a quick prayer. Every time your phone dings? Whisper, "God, guide me."

- **Prayer Journal**
  Write your prayers like letters to God. It helps you stay focused and gives you something to look back on—your own story of God's faithfulness.

o   **Worship First**
    Sometimes you don't have words. That's okay. Listen to a worship song and let that be your prayer. Let God meet you there.

o   **End-of-Day Check-In**
    Before bed, take a few minutes to thank God for the day and talk through anything on your heart. It's a great way to release the stress and rest in His peace.

 Key Scriptures

James 5:16 (NIV)
"The prayer of a righteous person is powerful and effective."

⇨   Your prayers matter. Even the short ones. Even the messy ones. God hears every word.

Philippians 4:6-7 (NIV)
"Do not be anxious about anything, but in every situation, by prayer and petition, with thanksgiving, present your requests to God. And the peace of God… will guard your hearts and your minds in Christ Jesus."

⇨   Prayer isn't just about asking—it's about replacing worry with peace.

Jeremiah 29:12-13 (NIV)
"Then you will call on Me and come and pray to Me, and I will listen to you. You will seek Me and find Me when you seek Me with all your heart."

⇨   God isn't hiding. He wants to be found. Just come close.

Romans 8:26 (NIV)
"…The Spirit Himself intercedes for us through wordless groans."

⇨   When you don't know what to say, the Holy Spirit speaks for you. You're never alone.

 # Journal Prompts

- o   When has prayer felt hard or awkward for me?

- o   What do I really want to talk to God about, but haven't?

- o   What might God be trying to say to me this week?

- o   How could I make prayer part of my daily rhythm?

This Week's Challenge

Start a prayer journal this week.
It doesn't have to be perfect. Just start writing like you're texting a best friend—
because that's how close God wants to be.

Try writing one prayer every day for seven days. At the end of the week, read
back and see what God might've been doing all along.

 ## Let's Pray

Dear God,

*Thank You that I don't have to have perfect words to come to You. Help me to be
real in my prayers—to talk to You, listen to You, and trust You. Teach me to pray
in a way that draws me closer to Your heart. Help me build a prayer life that's
honest, personal, and full of faith. I want to know You more.*

In Jesus name,
Amen

## Chapter 47

Daily Faith Habits That Actually Work
Prayer, Scripture, worship, and finding your rhythm

"Remain in me, as I also remain in you."
— **John 15:4 (NIV)**

Faith Doesn't Grow by Accident

Let's be honest—when life gets busy (school, sports, social stuff, scrolling), faith habits are usually the first to get shoved to the side.

We know prayer is important. We know we should read the Bible. We love worship—especially that one song that hits hard—but some days... it's just hard to stay consistent.

Here's the good news: *God isn't looking for perfect habits. He's looking for a connected heart.*

This chapter is all about building daily faith rhythms that are *realistic, meaningful,* and totally doable in your everyday life—even when things get chaotic.

Faith Grows in the Daily

Just like you can't grow strong muscles without showing up to the gym (ugh, we know), you can't grow deep faith without daily connection to Jesus.

Not performance.
Not perfection.
Just *presence*.

The goal isn't to check boxes on a "Good Christian Girl" list. The goal is to stay close to Jesus. And the best way to do that? Build rhythms that help you hear His voice, feel His love, and trust Him more.

What Are Daily Faith Habits?

They're simply small practices you do on purpose to draw closer to God. Think of them like soul workouts—gentle, steady, powerful. Here are four habits that actually work:

1. Scripture: Letting God Speak First

The Bible isn't just an old book with cool stories. It's God's voice in written form. When you read it, you're not just learning—you're listening.

And here's a little secret: you don't have to read 10 chapters a day. Even one verse can change your whole outlook.

Start small:

> Read a Psalm each morning.
>
> Choose a verse to write on a sticky note and stick it to your mirror.
>
> Use a Bible app plan that fits your season (tons are made just for teen girls!).

"Your word is a lamp to my feet and a light to my path."
— Psalm 119:105 (NIV)

2. Pray, Talk and Listen

Prayer doesn't need fancy words. It just needs you.

Talk to God like you'd talk to your best friend. Tell Him what's on your mind, ask for help, say thank you, and—this one's tough—make space to listen.

Ideas to try:

o   Keep a prayer journal

o   Try "breath prayers" (short phrases you say as you breathe in and out, like "God, I trust You")

o   Pause before bed to thank Him for something good from the day

"Pray continually."
— 1 Thessalonians 5:17 (NIV)

3. Worship: Shift the Atmosphere

Worship isn't just singing—though yes, your favorite Jesus jams totally count. Worship is anytime you put your heart and focus on God. It can change the mood of your day in seconds.

Try this:

o   Play worship music while getting ready or doing homework

o   Journal your praise to God

o   Dance it out in your room (yes, really)

"Come, let us sing for joy to the Lord... let us bow down in worship."
— Psalm 95:1,6 (NIV)

4. Find Your Faith Rhythm

Everyone's schedule is different. Maybe your mornings are chaos but your nights are quiet. Maybe weekends give you more space.

That's okay. The key is to find a *rhythm*—not a rigid rulebook—that fits how God made you.

Some ideas:

o   5 minutes in the morning: Scripture + short prayer

o   Worship during a walk

o   One journaling night a week

o   Prayer breaks between classes

You don't have to do everything every day. Pick what works, and grow from there. Faith is a *journey*, not a to-do list.

"Draw near to God and He will draw near to you."
— **James 4:8 (NIV)**

Real Faith, Real Life

Faith habits aren't meant to feel forced. They're meant to *fuel* your life. When you spend time with Jesus consistently, even in small ways, you'll notice:

- o   More peace, less pressure
- o   Stronger confidence
- o   Closer connection to God's voice
- o   A heart that's rooted, not shaken

It's not about how much time you spend. It's about being *present* when you do. Even a few minutes a day can make a big difference.

  Key Scriptures

John 15:4 (NIV)
"Remain in me, as I also remain in you."

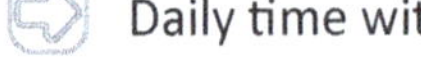   Stay close. That's the point of it all.

Romans 12:2 (NIV)
"Do not conform to the pattern of this world, but be transformed by the renewing of your mind."

  Daily time with God renews your mind and shifts your perspective.

Isaiah 40:31 (NIV)
"But those who hope in the Lord will renew their strength."

  Faith habits refill your strength, especially when you feel empty.

Psalm 63:1 (NIV)
"You, God, are my God, earnestly I seek you... I thirst for you."

   Your soul longs for God. Feed it with time in His presence.

Journal Prompts

- o   What part of my day feels like the best time to connect with God?

- o   Which of the four habits do I naturally lean toward? Which one feels harder?

- o   How can I build small, meaningful faith moments into my routine this week?

- o   What's one thing I've learned from God lately during my quiet time?

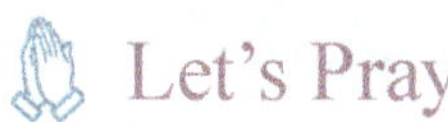

This Week's Challenge

Pick one habit to practice for 7 days. Just one. Keep it simple and commit to showing up daily, even if it's just five minutes. After a week, reflect: How did it shape your mood, your thoughts, or your connection with God?

Let's Pray

Jesus,

Help me stay close to You—not just on Sundays or when things feel hard, but every day. Show me how to build rhythms that bring me peace, strength, and joy in You. I don't want to go through life on empty. I want to live rooted in You. Thank You for wanting to spend time with me. I'm showing up, and I know You will too.

Thank you,
Amen

## Chapter 48

You're a Leader (Whether You Feel Like It or Not)

How to influence others without a platform

"Don't let anyone look down on you because you are young, but set an example for the believers in speech, in conduct, in love, in faith and in purity."
— 1 Timothy 4:12 (NIV)

Wait... Me? A Leader?

If your first thought is, *"I'm not a leader—I'm just trying to get through school and figure out my life,"*—you're not alone.

It's easy to think leadership is reserved for the people with thousands of followers, a microphone in their hand, or a title next to their name. But here's the truth: *Leadership isn't about position. It's about influence.*

And *everyone* influences someone.
Yes—even you.

Whether you realize it or not, people are watching how you live. Friends. Siblings. Classmates. That kid who sits two rows behind you in math. You don't need a platform to lead. You just need to live your life in a way that points to something (or Someone) greater.

You Lead by How You Live

Let's flip the script on leadership. What if it's not about having it all figured out or being the loudest in the room, but about:

o   Choosing kindness when it's easier to be cold

o   Speaking life instead of gossip

o   Standing for truth even when it's uncomfortable

o   Offering a listening ear instead of quick advice

o   Being *present*, *authentic*, and *real* in a world full of filters

That's leadership. Quiet, consistent, courageous leadership.

What Leadership Really Looks Like

Let's break it down. Here's how you can lead—right where you are:

1. In Speech

Your words carry weight. They can either build up or tear down. Choose to speak hope, encouragement, and truth.

Ask yourself: *Are my words bringing life or draining it?*

2. In Conduct

People watch what you do, not just what you say. Your actions preach louder than any caption.

Are you living with integrity, even when no one's looking?

3. In Love

Love looks like inclusion. Like sitting with someone who's alone. Like giving grace when someone messes up. It's not mushy—it's powerful.

How can you show love today in a practical way?

4. In Faith

You don't have to be the most "spiritual" person in the room to walk in faith. Just keep trusting Jesus and letting others see that trust in action.

How do you respond when life doesn't go your way? That's faith on display.

5. In Purity

This isn't just about relationships. It's about living with intention and clarity—having a heart that's set apart and not chasing everything culture throws at you.

Are you letting your life be led by purpose or pressure?

You Don't Need a Stage to Be Significant

Some of the most impactful leaders are the ones no one sees. Think of the quiet girl who always remembers your birthday. Or the friend who checks in when no one else does. Or the youth leader who listens more than she talks.

God doesn't just use the popular. He uses the available.

Jesus picked fishermen and tax collectors—not celebrities. His own leadership looked like serving, not spotlight.

So if you feel invisible or unqualified—good news. You're exactly the kind of person God loves to work through.

 Key Scriptures

1 Timothy 4:12 (NIV)
"Don't let anyone look down on you because you are young, but set an example…"

 Your age isn't a limitation—it's an opportunity.

Matthew 23:11 (NLT)
"The greatest among you must be a servant."

 True leaders serve first.

Proverbs 11:25 (NIV)
"A generous person will prosper; whoever refreshes others will be refreshed."

 Pouring into others blesses you too.

Galatians 6:9 (NIV)

"Let us not become weary in doing good, for at the proper time we will reap a harvest if we do not give up."

 Keep leading with faithfulness—even if no one applauds.

Journal Prompts

- o   Who in my life might be watching how I live—even if I don't realize it?

- o   What kind of leader do I want to be known as?

- o   Which area of 1 Timothy 4:12 (speech, conduct, love, faith, purity) do I want to grow in?

- o   How can I lead without needing to be loud?

This Week's Challenge

This week, pick one small way to lead by example. Maybe it's encouraging a friend, inviting someone new into your circle, or starting your day with prayer instead of panic. Ask God to help you notice opportunities to lead—not with spotlight, but with *substance*.

 Let's Pray

Dear Heavenly Father,

sometimes I don't feel like a leader. I feel too young, too quiet, too unsure. But I believe You've placed me here on purpose. Help me lead with love, with truth, and with confidence that comes from You—not from likes, labels, or followers. Show me how to be an example, even when no one's watching. I want to make You known by how I live.

In Jesus name,
Amen.

## Chapter 49

God Doesn't Waste Anything
Turning Struggles into Testimonies

"And we know that in all things God works for the good of those who love him, who have been called according to his purpose."
— Romans 8:28 (NIV)

The Pain That Feels Pointless

Let's be honest—some seasons just hurt. There are moments in life when everything feels upside down, and it seems like no one really gets what you're going through. Maybe your heart feels like it's been shattered into pieces after a friendship breakup, or maybe you're battling anxiety and don't even know why. Or maybe you've been trying to hold it all together for so long that you're just...tired.

When you're in the middle of that kind of struggle, it's so easy to wonder, *Where is God in all of this?* It can feel like He's gone quiet—or worse, that He's left the chat.

But here's the truth: just because you don't feel God doesn't mean He isn't
working. He's not ignoring your pain. He's sitting right there in it with you.

And here's the even crazier part? That pain you're walking through right now...God can use it for something bigger than you could imagine. It might not make sense right away (or for a long time), but not a single moment of it will be wasted.
Not the tears. Not the prayers. Not the hard questions. Not even the parts you wish you could erase.

God is in the business of making broken things beautiful—and that includes your story.

From Mess to Message

There's this thing God does that's kind of wild—He takes what feels like a *mess* and turns it into a message.

Think of your life like a piece of stained glass. Up close, all you can see are the sharp, jagged edges. Some are dark, some are shattered, and it's hard to picture how anything beautiful could come from it. But when the light shines through those broken pieces? Wow. A masterpiece.

That's what God does. He shines His light through your brokenness to show others His beauty, His healing, and His hope.

Your struggles don't disqualify you from being used by God—they *prepare* you. They give you compassion. They build your faith. They make you relatable. And most of all, they remind you that your strength doesn't come from having it all together—but from knowing the One who does.

You don't have to wait until you've "arrived" to be used by God. You just have to be willing to say, *"Okay, Lord. I don't get it right now, but I give it to You."*

Because your story—even the messy middle—can help someone else feel seen, understood, and not so alone.

Your Story Isn't Over

When you're hurting, it can feel like this is the end of your story. Like you've failed, messed up too bad, or that nothing good could possibly come from this chapter.

But girl—this isn't the end. It's just a plot twist.

God is still writing. And He's not just a good writer; He's the Author of your story, and He sees the big picture even when all you see is the page you're stuck on.

There's this pressure to have a neat, tied-up-in-a-bow kind of testimony, right? But real testimonies are raw. They're honest. They include the waiting, the tears, and the "I'm still figuring this out" moments. You don't have to be fully healed or fully confident to be used by God—you just need to be real and open.

When you share how God is meeting you in your struggles—*even before the happy ending*—you invite others to do the same. You become a lighthouse, not because your life is perfect, but because you've decided to shine anyway.

 Key Scriptures

Romans 8:28 (NIV)
"And we know that in all things God works for the good of those who love him..."

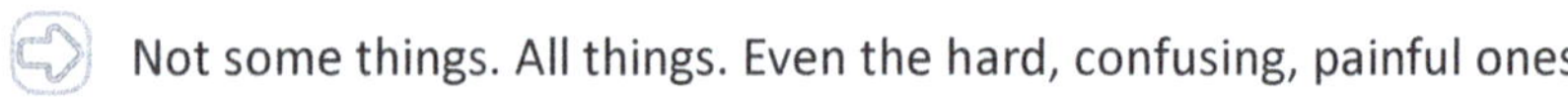 Not some things. All things. Even the hard, confusing, painful ones.

2 Corinthians 1:3–4 (NLT)
"He comforts us in all our troubles so that we can comfort others..."

Your healing becomes someone else's hope.

Genesis 50:20 (NIV)
"You intended to harm me, but God intended it for good..."

What was meant to break you can actually build you.

Isaiah 61:3 (NIV)
"...to bestow on them a crown of beauty instead of ashes..."

God brings beauty out of what feels burned and broken.

Journal Prompts

- o   What is one struggle or hard season I've walked through that still feels confusing or painful?

- o   Can I see any ways God has used that experience for good—or might use it in the future?

- o   Who in my life could be encouraged by my story, even if it's still unfinished?

- o   What would it look like to trust God *right in the middle* of my pain?

This Week's Challenge

This week, take a moment to write down a part of your story that has been difficult. Don't worry about making it sound perfect. Just be real. Then, ask God to show you how He might use it—for your growth, for someone else's encouragement, or as a deeper part of your faith walk.

And if you feel brave, share it. With a friend. In a journal. Maybe even online.
You never know who needs to hear that they're not alone.

Let's Pray

Dear Heavenly Father,

sometimes it's hard to believe that You can use my pain for anything good. But I trust that You are a Redeemer, a Restorer, a God who brings beauty from ashes. Help me to see my story through Your eyes. Use my struggles to bring hope to others, and remind me that nothing I've been through is wasted in Your hands.

In Jesus name,
Amen.

## Chapter 50

Be the Light

Living boldly in a world that tells you to shrink
Matthew 5:14–16 (NIV)

The Pressure to Dim Down

Let's talk about the pressure to *shrink*.

You know what I mean—that sneaky voice in your head that says, "Don't be too loud about your faith," or "If you stand out too much, people might think you're weird." It shows up when you're about to pray before lunch in public or when a teacher brings up controversial topics and your heart races because you know where you stand—but you're scared to say it out loud.

The truth is, the world has a subtle (and sometimes not-so-subtle) way of convincing you to blend in. Culture promotes a version of "acceptance" that often means staying silent about your convictions. It praises individuality—until your values don't match what's trending.

But Jesus didn't call you to be quiet about your faith. He didn't say, "Stay hidden until it's safe." He said *you are the light of the world*. Not you could be or maybe one day—you are. Right now. Right where you are. That means your story, your presence, your kindness, your courage—they all carry light.

The world needs your light. And more than that, God *placed* you here on purpose to shine.

Living Out Loud (Without Being Loud) (Expanded)

Let's clear up a big misconception: *bold faith* doesn't always mean *loud faith*.

You don't need a microphone, a YouTube channel, or a viral reel to make an impact (though if that's your calling, go for it!). Living out loud is more about *consistency than volume*. It's about who you are when no one is watching—and how that matches who you are when everyone is.

Living your faith out loud might look like:

- o   Choosing forgiveness when it's easier to hold a grudge.

- o   Refusing to gossip, even if everyone else is doing it.

- o   Offering a kind word or prayer to someone who's having a rough day.

- o   Standing up for someone who's being excluded or bullied.

These things may not seem huge in the moment, but they're acts of light. And light spreads.

You're not responsible for saving the world. You're responsible for showing up faithfully, loving people like Jesus did, and trusting that God will use your life—even the quiet parts—for His glory.

Remember: you don't have to shout to shine. Your faith can be bold, steady, and powerful without ever making a scene.

Don't Hide Your Fire (Expanded)

Have you ever walked into a dark room and immediately reached for your phone flashlight? Even a tiny bit of light makes a huge difference in the dark.

That's you.

The enemy would love for you to believe that your voice is too small, your story too messy, your prayers too simple, or your faith not "Christian enough." But here's what's true: *God is glorified when you choose to shine anyway.*

When you hide your fire—your gifts, your faith, your uniqueness—you're not just protecting yourself from judgment. You're also withholding the light someone else might desperately need. What if someone is praying for the hope that *you* carry? What if your encouragement, your quiet strength, your testimony is exactly what points them to Jesus?

Hiding might feel safer, but it's not where you thrive. You were made to glow. Not in a self-glorifying way, but in a way that reflects the brilliance of the One who created you.

You don't have to be perfect to shine—just *willing*.

Fueling Your Fire (Expanded)

Have you ever tried to light a candle that's been snuffed out for a while? The wick is there, but it's dry. It takes time, heat, and a steady flame to bring it back to life.

That's what happens when you try to shine without staying connected to the Source—Jesus.

You might be trying to be a good person, serve others, or be kind at school, but if you're running on empty spiritually, your flame can flicker fast. Just like your phone needs to stay charged, your spirit needs daily connection with God.

So how do you fuel your fire?

- o **Spend time in Scripture.** Even a few verses a day can reset your mind and remind you of who you are in Christ.

- o **Pray consistently.** Talk to God honestly. Bring Him your highs, lows, and awkward in-betweens. He's listening.

- o **Worship.** Whether it's during church or in your headphones while doing homework, worship invites God's presence and refreshes your heart.

- o **Surround yourself with community.** Friends who build you up in your faith will help your light burn brighter and steadier.

When you stay close to God, He fills you with light—and that light becomes impossible to ignore.

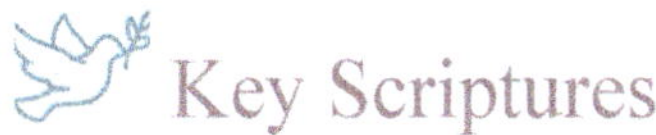 # Key Scriptures

1. Matthew 5:14–16 (NIV)

"You are the light of the world. A town built on a hill cannot be hidden. Neither do people light a lamp and put it under a bowl. Instead, they put it on its stand, and it gives light to everyone in the house. In the same way, let your light shine before others, that they may see your good deeds and glorify your Father in heaven."

Let's unpack this:

Jesus isn't just giving you a compliment here—He's giving you an assignment. When He says *"you are the light of the world,"* He's saying that your life is meant to shine, to stand out in love, truth, and compassion in a world that can often feel dark, confusing, or cruel.

But here's the part we sometimes miss: *light doesn't brag about being light. It just shines.* You don't have to force it. Just live in a way that reflects God's heart—kindness, courage, honesty, humility—and others will see it.

Real-life example: When someone is gossiping at lunch, and you choose to speak up kindly or change the subject—*you're being a light.* When you help a struggling classmate even though no one else notices—*you're shining.*

And guess what? That kind of light brings *glory to God,* not just good vibes.

2. Philippians 2:15 (NLT)

"Live clean, innocent lives as children of God, shining like bright lights in a world full of crooked and perverse people."

Here's what it means:

This verse isn't saying you need to be *perfect.* It's saying that your life should reflect your relationship with God—even when the world is heading in the opposite direction. "Clean" and "innocent" doesn't mean boring—it means *set apart.* It means choosing honesty over shortcuts, kindness over cliques, purity over popularity.

Application: It's easy to follow the crowd, especially when it seems like everyone's doing whatever feels good or popular. But when you choose to honor God with your decisions, you *shine*. You stand out in the best kind of way—like a star in a dark sky. And people will notice, even if they don't say it out loud.

3. Romans 12:2 (NIV)

"Do not conform to the pattern of this world, but be transformed by the renewing of your mind. Then you will be able to test and approve what God's will is—his good, pleasing and perfect will."

What this means for you:

It's tempting to blend in. Social media, friend groups, and culture often send the message that you need to act or look a certain way to matter. But Paul is saying: *Don't copy the culture.* Don't squeeze into a mold that was never meant for you.

Instead, let God transform how you think. That starts by spending time in His Word, in prayer, and surrounding yourself with people who help you grow, not shrink. As your mind is renewed, your boldness grows too—and suddenly, you're no longer swayed by every opinion or trend.

Real-life application: Next time you're feeling insecure because everyone else seems more confident, prettier, or successful, stop and ask: *Is that God's voice, or the world's pressure?* Then remind yourself of what God says about you—you are chosen, loved, and called to be light.

4. 2 Timothy 1:7 (NLT)

"For God has not given us a spirit of fear and timidity, but of power, love, and self-discipline."

Here's why this matters:

Boldness doesn't mean being loud or fearless all the time. But it does mean we don't let fear be the boss of us. God hasn't given you a fearful spirit— He's given you *power, love,* and *self-discipline.* That's your spiritual toolkit for courage.

Everyday application: The next time you feel nervous to pray out loud, post something about your faith, or invite a friend to church—pause, take a deep breath, and remember: *God is in you. Fear isn't your identity—faith is.*

5. Isaiah 60:1 (NIV)

"Arise, shine, for your light has come, and the glory of the Lord rises upon you."

What this means for your journey:

This is your wake-up call. *Get up. Shine on.* Not in your own strength, but because *God's glory is on you.* You're not trying to create light—you already have it. Jesus lives in you. So walk confidently, not because you're perfect, but because *His presence goes before you.*

Daily practice: Start your day by praying, "God, help me shine today. Not for attention, but so that others can see You in me." That's how light becomes contagious.

Journal Prompts

- o   Where in your life do you feel pressure to dim your light?

- o   What does "being a light" look like in your school, family, or online presence?

- o   How can you stay fueled spiritually so your light doesn't fade?

This Week's Challenge

Do one bold thing that reflects God's love this week—whether it's inviting someone to youth group, encouraging a struggling friend, or posting something faith-filled online. One spark can inspire a whole room.

 # Let's Pray

Dear God,

Thank You for calling me to shine in a world that needs Your light. Help me to be bold, not because I'm confident in myself, but because I trust in You. When I feel afraid to stand out, remind me that I'm never alone. Keep my heart steady, my light bright, and my focus on You. Let others see Your love in me.

In Jesus name,
Amen